Antonija Mežnarić

WHAT DO NIGHTMARES DREAM OF

SHTRIGA

What do Nightmares Dream of

Publisher: Shtriga

ISBN
epub 978-953-8360-02-2
mobi 978-953-8360-03-9
print 978-953-8360-06-0

Author: Antonija Mežnarić
Edited by: Vesna Kurilić
Cover design: Antonija Mežnarić, based on images by Daria Shevtsova and Kristina Nor at Pexels

Published in Rijeka, 2020.

First edition

shtriga.com
shtrigabooks@gmail.com
@shtrigabooks

Content warning:
mentions of child abuse
mentions of suicide

1

It was raining—which was nothing unusual, only slightly distracting—when the ear-shattering scream exploded all around Sanja. Instinctively, her hands flew to cover her ears, but the wailing was so loud it resonated inside her head. *This can't be happening*, she thought, and yet, unfathomably, it was.

Sanja was in the middle of grading papers—descriptions of family members by her sixth graders—tired of everything, but mostly of the latest gibberish that had gotten under her hands. She had troubles staying awake with the constant flow of rain doing its very best to lull her into sleep.

Then, without warning, the question marks written in red ink started screaming at her from the page as if she were somehow torturing the paper with her pen. The inky letters describing blue and green and brown eyes of various family members started crawling across the page like a hundred ants. *What the fuck, what's happening?* Sanja rubbed her eyes, confused as to why words would try to run away. If they'd managed to do that, they would have infested this world with their lazy writing, sucking out all creativity and the will to live from children.

She closed the child's notebook before it could happen, only to see it start rapidly inflating, as if drying out after being left in the rain. Slowly, Sanja stood up and started moving away from the desk, not sure what she should even do in this sort of situation. Burn the notebooks? Grade them, bound them in chains—where would she get the chains—or run away, quit her job and become a nun? Just like one of those recluse ones, who are forbidden to interact with the world, so that everyone would leave her alone?

Her skin was prickling. The view outside her window had been replaced with pitch black darkness. Which didn't make much sense because it was still early in the day. But she couldn't really be sure, unable to think with all the screaming which was getting louder and louder. What will her neighbours think? It sounded like she was torturing someone, and the last thing she needed were cops at the door because her papers didn't want to be read and graded. How could she explain that?

While she was just standing there, doing nothing at all, the puffy notebook exploded on the desk surface. Tiny bits of shredded paper floated in the air like gutted insides of a fish, ending up all over Sanja's head, shoulders and toes. They crawled all over her, these tiny ants made of ink, burrowing inside her skin, even going inside her mouth, clogging her throat before she could start screaming. Her legs felt stuck to the floor, and no matter how much she flailed with her arms, she couldn't get rid of the words attacking her.

Finally, she could feel them settling in her lungs. She was coughing out ink now, like a cat would a furball, but a big lump had gotten stuck in her trachea. Desperately, she started clawing at the skin of her throat with her short nails, trying to make way for the air with her own fingers, even though part of her knew it was a futile work. It hurt like hell and she could feel the words in her lungs, walking all over her organ tissue on sharp legs, puncturing holes wherever they went. She couldn't die so young, not over something as stupid as a school assignment, over an utterly boring description of a family member!

A light bulb turned on in her head and she jerked awake as if she'd been dropped down from thin air into a chair. She snapped in front of a very silent, still-looking piece of paper spotted with ink and saliva—because, apparently, she had been drooling on top of it while she was sleeping.

"Goddamnit! I'm trying to work!" Sanja shouted out into the air around her. "You know that, if I don't finish this soon, the kids will eat me alive. They hate writing assignments, they hate my subject, they halfass everything I give them because they don't care. But still, if I don't grade the papers, like, at this same minute, they absolutely will crucify me. So. Leave. Me. The. Fuck. Alone."

She was shaking but she didn't care. There was still a bunch of work to be done and she'll probably squint over it late into the night, so there was no room for fear, only anger brought on by being tricked into falling asleep and making her live through some cheap nightmare, worthy of a B-rated horror movie.

"You know, your nightmares are as lazy as the writing my students do. And they are kids! What is your excuse?" Sanja was still arguing with the air around her—not expecting her unwelcome roommate to give her any sort of answer—because she needed to get it off her chest. Also, she probably shouldn't be taunting evil entities, but fuck it if she wasn't simmering with rage. They'd made her drool all over a student's paper—so unprofessional!

"Don't you have anything to say for yourself?" she as good as screamed. "It's just that, if you don't have anything smart to terrorise me with, at least be decent enough to wait for nighttime and after I've fallen asleep in my bed, okay?"

There was no answer, of course. Only a small, but certain feeling of a presence looming behind her back. And, possibly, glaring daggers at her head.

"You know what, I think this kind of behavior warrants punishment. Don't you agree?"

She couldn't ignore this thing. It wasn't the sort of thing she wanted to encourage with her lack of counteraction. It made her wonder if a certain cousin of hers had time to visit with her this weekend.

"I think it's time for Shimun to drop by," she said out loud and smiled when she heard a loud, incorporeal hiss right by her ear.

* * *

At first she'd thought the only thing that plagued her were the nightmares.

It started a few nights after she'd moved into the new apartment. Nothing special, in the beginning; she would just wake up in the middle of the night after an unsettling dream, its content fading away with every passing moment. And it wasn't like it happened every night. But then the intensity started to increase. Nightmares became more vivid, and with their monstruos clarity came a deep sense of dread which would follow her into consciousness. Sanja would startle awake, only to find out she couldn't move an inch of her body. Completely paralysed, she would freak out until, ever so slightly, the pressure on her body would finally pass away and she would reclaim her movement. Sometimes it felt like her dreams had tried to choke her to death and she would rouse with a hoarse throat, like she'd screamed all night.

Nevertheless, it didn't concern her too much. She had too much emotional baggage to be in any way surprised that some of it found a way to burst out during the night. Sanja didn't really spare much thought for her night terrors, not until the night she woke up from her nightmare—her oldest uncle trying to bury her alive—to the shape of a person standing by her bed. Watching her. Scrambling for her nightlight, her heart almost lept from her chest, but when light finally flooded the room there was no one there. And yet she felt like she was watched. And it didn't stop.

Some would blame it on sleep paralysis. Some would book an appointment with a therapist. But not her. Sanja came to an easy conclusion that there was something supernatural at play. Easy, for her, because she was raised to believe in things most people wouldn't—ghosts that visited their beloveds, demon possessions, werewolves (but not vampires, she had to draw a line somewhere). With her childhood in mind, she learned how to recognise the signs of her invisible roommate. She was also sure that it—whatever it was supposed to be—was behind her nightmares.

She just had to learn what exactly was tormenting her. It was the first step in finding a way of dealing with it. Googling her symptoms without any starting theories ended with so many possibilities, including but not limited to PTSD, sleep paralysis and, of course, some type of cancer. And after that it was demons. But she wasn't overtly sold on that, even with a lot of hints pointing in that direction. In the meantime, while she was trying to find a more credible source, she learned that one thing could be very helpful.

And it revolved around her cousin, who very much leaned to the demonic possession explanation.

* * *

"Please, for the love of all that is holy, just move out." Shimun, Sanja's first cousin on her mother's side, was sitting on the edge of the couch, visibly upset.

He wore what he called his 'civilian clothes'; a warm-looking brown sweater over a white button down and a pair of hipster, plaid pants in wool—instead of an all black wardrobe which made him look like a Night's Watchman—and sans his clerical collar.

Sanja was just pouring them both some of the altar wine that her cousin had so generously brought. Almost double the dose for herself, even though it was starting to look like her cousin might need it more.

"Why? I have the best view in the city," Sanja handed him the glass and pointed at the tall windows. It was hard to see through the heavy rain bathing her view in a washed up industrial grey, but, below her apartment on the seventh floor, you could see a line of old, decaying houses with wet red roofs. In the distance, the rusty blue and dark yellow wagons of a cargo train lay on the railway track. Beyond them, the port warehouses stood with their prized jewel, the Metropolis building in all its towering theatrical glory. Nowadays, all it served for was to remind everyone that, once upon a time, this town had style.

Even further, behind the Metropolis and port's garbage disposal, was the stirred up sea, the colour of dark ash, connecting to the sky. During the storms, or rainy days like these, it was impossible to say where the sea ended or the sky started.

"Sanja, this place is cursed. Forget about the view, you are living with the damned," Shimun's voice was high pitched, sounding scratchy to her ears. She shrugged and dragged her eyes away from the view. No matter how beautiful it was, she was actually lying through her teeth about how much it enticed her. Her flat was too high in the building. That was the problem. She was on the *seventh* floor, and watching outside made her taste the bile.

But she couldn't afford to be too picky when buying her own place, so she just had to learn to live with this vast emptiness outside her windows, and the fact that the windowsill started just below the line of her hips, which would made it so easy to just slip and fall to her death outside.

"It wouldn't be my first time to live with demons. Remember growing up with Grandma?" Sanja knew he wouldn't appreciate the joke but she had to tell it anyway.

"That was horrible, don't talk like that." Her cousin really didn't have a sense of humour. It was probably why he'd become a catholic priest in the first place.

She sat down across from him, on a small chair below the window. Like this, she couldn't see outside, but she could watch her cousin's unamused face. "Whyever not? It's true."

She could still feel all the places on her body where the crop-like walnut branch had hit her during that time, a deep rooted shame tingling with every hit. It was a long time ago, but her body still remembered.

"Good old times when you could get beaten up to a pulp because you'd gone on a stroll through the village alongside the only other girl your age, because *somehow* that made you a loose woman, and people would *talk*... Or, I guess you wouldn't, because you never were restricted to the house. Your perspective on our childhood and mine are quite different." Sanja took a big gulp of wine, enjoying how its bitterness matched her own. He couldn't understand, she knew it fully well. He never had to live with grandma full time. The summertimes, when the three of them would go together on vacation at grandma's childhood home in a small, inconsequential village near the sea, wasn't as strictly regulated to him as to her. And that was only at their summer house. It was even worse for her when they got home. Unlike him—who got to go back to his parents—she couldn't get away. Even while her mother was still alive, they were both stuck with Grandma.

"It's not fair, Sanja, it really isn't. I got my share of the beatings, too. But still, it was a different time, different upbringing. Our grandma had to kneel on dry corn kernels in school if she'd misbehaved or didn't know the answer. Which is an educational method that I believe is not in use anymore. Because times have changed."

"And a pity for that. Some of the kids could surely benefit from those methods." Already a few names were springing to her mind.

“You have a dark sense of humor, Sanja.”

“Better than none.”

“Har har,” Shimun said dryly, illustrating her point. “Listen, can we be serious for a moment? Why don’t you want to move out?” She could read the silent plea in his eyes, sad and gray like the sea outside. Her cousin cared, he always did, which was why she trusted him with this.

“We can’t all be priests, Shimun, having all our needs taken care of. I live on a teacher’s salary. Do you know what that means? Even with the bank loan I didn’t have the budget for anything even remotely safe which wasn’t also a depressing dump of a hole with moldy walls. This was the best place I could get. It’s spacious and it came with relatively small issues that needed fixing, not to mention all the furnishing I got with the apartment. It was a great deal, it still is.”

Saying it aloud right now made her think she should have known something was amiss with this apartment. It had been cheap, even though it had two bedrooms, a small kitchen adjacent to the dining room, and a separate living room. But she was too focused on the fact that she could afford it, and instantly started daydreaming of turning the smaller bedroom into a studio and the dining room into a home office. She hadn’t really thought a lot about why a place this big would be priced so low, especially when other smaller appartements were pricier.

“You have a weird definition of a ‘great deal’, given that it’s haunted.”

“Technically, we’re not sure if the place is haunted or *I*.”

“It started when you moved here! Even I can feel its presence.” He shook slightly all over to demonstrate his point—or because he was feeling the cold seeping in with the rain and the wind through the cracks in the window pane. The flat was great, but it still needed some fixing up, and old windows with broken glass should be the first big thing to go. It was a shame she had no money for new ones... but that's what warm clothes and blankets are for.

"I can't afford to move to a new place. I'm still paying back the loan, I'll be doing that for the next *thirty years*. Listen to me carefully," she said and raised her glass. "I invested everything I had in this place, I don't have the money to move out just because it has a... supernatural pest problem. Especially if that problem decides to follow me. If it's haunting me and not the place, it really isn't important where I live, is it?"

"You could always move back—"

"Do not finish that sentence, don't you dare!" Now it was him who was irritating her. Even suggesting something like that, only minutes after she'd clearly stated what she thought of their grandmother. Sanja drank a good portion of the wine again, just to stop herself from flinging the glass with its contents right into Shimun's face.

"Okay, okay, sorry. Still, I worry. What if it kills you?"

He just cared for her, she had to remind herself of that. Like he did when he lied to their grandmother thousands of times, covering for her during their childhood. To help her go on school trips or spend time in the library after school; even when she'd simply wanted to play with her friends—those few friends she'd had who wanted to hang out with her. Shimun had even given her his own pocket money when she had none, and bought new sneakers so the other school kids wouldn't make fun of her for being so out of date with everything she owned just because Grandma was strict, in every sense of that word. He'd always had her back, and Sanja's childhood would have been a thousand times worse if it hadn't been for him.

"Nicotine kills, and people still smoke of their own volition."

"Not the same," he sighed, looking as if she'd drained him of all his strength through the last few minutes of their conversation. There was sadness and worry drawn in the lines of his face, almost like a painter had wanted to show someone accustomed to sorrow buried deep inside a locked treasure chest. Only there were no gems and gold there, but rather tears and loneliness.

She shook her head, trying to clear it of sudden melancholic thoughts. “Just read, please. That’s why I called you here. It helps, really, it annoys the *thing* to no end. I’m managing, don’t be afraid. It’s what the angels say, isn’t it? ‘Don’t be afraid.’”

“Why wouldn’t you at least let me bless the apartment?”

“Absolutely not,” she recoiled. “I need to live here too.”

“Sanja, it wouldn’t banish *you*,” he sounded more than exasperated with her behavior, but it wasn’t like he could relate. He was a *priest*, which meant he had a fundamentally different view on institutionalised religion from her. But there was no way in hell she’ll wittingly live in one of those houses marked with little stickers of Virgin Mary and Jesus stuck to the door frames, supposedly keeping her safe. Like the flat which she’d grown up in; and yet none of the figures pictured could do anything about her misfortunes. Instead they were used as an excuse to pile even more rules onto her. She couldn’t choose the storey for her flat, but she could choose not to be part of this ritual, or a part of the catholic Church.

“You’re not blessing my *home*, you’re not blessing *me*. Just *read*.”

Shimun shrugged, apparently devoid of words or the will for arguing on. Maybe, though, he simply knew there was nothing he could say or do to change her mind, so he would do the only thing which could help.

He opened the huge book in his lap, the one Sanja absolutely hated—but not as much as the creature did—and started reading the familiar words aloud.

Sanja got up and looked through the window, hearing her cousin’s high voice, pronouncing rhythmic biblical verses, merging with the clicking sound of her clock and the city outside: cars driving through puddles, braking suddenly, raindrops hitting roofs, trees, oily asphalt and glass panes. Her windows were crying, droplets slowly slipping, leaving their liquid trail. She closed her eyes and let the words mash up, ignoring their meaning and simply enjoying the moment of calm they created. There was no presence hissing behind her back, no nightmares. There were only her and her cousin, drinking bitter altar wine, painted in dusky colors. Still and serene on the background of her view of a dying industrial complex and the hungry sea, devouring the sky.

2

Everything was dark grey, from her thoughts to the weather typical for autumn in Rijeka.

Sanja picked up the pace, wanting to get to her car before rain started pouring down like Judgment Day. Her school didn't have its own parking lot, and the closest one not charging a fee was in an old, partially abandoned industrial part of the city that looked like a serial killer's dumping ground. Not ideal, but free. It also had a few living businesses—a coffee place, of course, although she would never set foot in there, being too fond of her organs to put them on the black market—a dry cleaner's, and a small grocery store for the few people that still lived in this street and the one above it. But mostly it was a graveyard for early twenty century factories.

She'd just finished her daily lectures and was dragging two dozen exams in her bag to grade at home, when she felt that she wasn't alone anymore on the dark lonely street.

There was a stranger walking behind her. It wasn't that odd, but he was a man, and she didn't see anyone else around. She was acutely aware of all the empty buildings where someone could drag her in, of broken glass littering the ground. The coffee shop and the store were already too far to get any help from there. It was silent except for the sound of the footsteps.

The chill crept through her body, so she started walking even faster, digging out her keys at the same time, consoling herself that everything would be alright, like it always was. But until she got in her car, parked next to a broken window of an abandoned factory down the street, she knew that the fist clenching her throat wouldn't relax.

She was soon at her car's door, when, out of the blue, a physical hand grabbed her from behind. She reeled and clenched her fist, ready to hit the offender, her heart jumping all the way to her throat and blocking the air, when she finally saw who it was. And stopped dead in her tracks.

"Dad?" It was such an unexpected sight that her bag dropped from her shoulder to the ground, papers slipping out into mud.

"What are you doing here? Jesus, you scared me!"

He had tears in his eyes and his hold of her was so strong it almost hurt.

"Dad, what's wrong?"

Wrinkles in his face and brown hair peppered with silver illustrated the old age he never got to experience, although she didn't remember how he looked anymore. Just that he had a beard, smoked a lot and was quite dashing and young.

"I'm sorry."

"For what? Dad?"

He was crying now, big fat tears streaming down his face. "I'm sorry. I'm just so, so hungry. I'm sorry."

And she saw it through the tears in her own eyes; fangs protruding from his mouth. His touch became steel, but she didn't even try to run. When the bite came down upon her throat it didn't even hurt. It just made it so, *so* hard to breathe and, with every drop of blood drained, it took even more effort to keep her eyes open and stay upright.

When her body dropped to the rain soaked ground, her fight abruptly ended as a scene cut in a movie. The grey city was replaced with the dark of her room, her father's vice-like grip of the dream with total paralysis in the waking world.

She saw her dad again. His hands had none of the scars; instead he got to age well, like fine wine. In this horrible twisted world of her nightmares, where nothing was real, he got to live.

She felt like she'd been crying with her whole body, lying in a bed sodden with bodily fluids, her face completely wet. With senses getting slowly reintroduced to her limbs, Sanja turned her teary eyes to the darkness and saw a figure standing at her bed. Unmoving shape, unmistakably human. It was there, close enough that she could stretch out her hand and touch it.

Her breath caught in her throat. But still, she blinked furiously through her tears and told the creature, "This was playing dirty. So, so low. Fuck you."

The shape didn't move. Didn't say a word. Sanja was done with it. She turned her back on it, stuck her face in the pillow and cried until there were no tears left and her throat was raw, feeling the presence behind her back all of the time.

Regardless, she fell asleep from exhaustion in the end and couldn't even be bothered to wake up even if the creature were stabbing her in the back.

* * *

The teacher's lounge during the lunch break was a place of cacophony and chaos, last minute preparations at the single computer and old copier, and venting frustrations. Sanja wasn't really interested in talking to her colleagues, so she decided to use her twenty minutes of peace to flip through the book she'd bought in the morning, before her first class, on the off chance it could contain some information pertaining to her situation. Finding the chapter which looked the most promising, she promptly ignored all of the noises around her, letting them disappear into the background.

“Hey, reading something interesting?” The question, annoyingly, was directed at her.

Sanja looked up from her book and saw Ana—the new math substitute teacher—standing close. There were vacant chairs at both Sanja’s sides and it looked like Ana wanted to use one, but thought better of it. That was a smart decision—the one on the left was the usual sitting place of a history teacher, and the one on the right of the biology professor, and both were known to get quite testy if someone else sat in their places. Well, most of the professors here were; the teacher’s lounge was not that different from the woods where everyone pissed around to mark their territory, with the possibility of a fight if someone transgressed. You had to tread carefully, especially if you were a new member of the faculty. And even though Ana had started working in their school the week before, she was obviously smart enough to catch up with where she could and couldn’t sit at the table.

Sanja shrugged, her heart beating a little bit faster all of a sudden. “Just something about fairies and other folk tale creatures, from the sites at Istra, Učka and this area,” she explained, just as a fight broke out between three teachers over who gets to use the copier first. It was loud and distracting, pounding all over her head.

“Huh.” Ana gave her a sunny smile that brightened up the whole room, and suddenly, the argument behind them became only white noise of a television stuck on a reality show program. “Is it for pleasure or work? Do you like reading fantasy? Because, I absolutely love reading fantasy and sci fi, but I thought you Croatian language teachers are mostly into mainstream and stuff, like...”

“Pretentious literature?” Sanja finished instead of her.

"Maybe. Sorry." Ana smiled sheepishly.

Sanja found herself smiling in return, feeling all warm and tingly inside. "Don't worry, I went to college with these people, I understand. But to answer your question, well, it's not for work, but I wouldn't call it pleasure either. It's the... Well, I'm not really a fantasy fan but I'm interested in the theory of it, the creatures from our great-grandparent's dark, I guess. Or, more specifically, folklore. In this particular case."

"Oh. And have you read something fun? Exciting? I know a few of our folk stories, like the one about the ox merchant who died and became a werewolf. He didn't really do anything but continue to sell the oxen until the angry mob found his grave and staked his heart. I always found it interesting how we conflated werewolves and vampires... But I'm rambling now. So? Is there a story you want to share with me? *Quid pro quo, Clarice.*" At that, Ana giggled at her own joke.

It was her chance, Sanja knew, but she wasn't certain for what, exactly. The new substitute caught her eye as soon as she'd started working at their school. It wasn't so surprising. Ana had the sort of energy that came with new teachers, an almost contagious enthusiasm. It was hard to miss her smile, like dawn bathing the sea in warm golden colors. Sanja's fingers always itched with need to paint her—as a siren sitting on a rock singing the lullaby, as a shimmering goddess lying in the high grass surrounded with roses and foxes. But she never did. Her paints kept drying out in their containers and the only thing that touched the canvas still waiting on its easel in her studio was dust.

No matter how much she wanted to approach Ana, there was always something holding her back. After their initial and brief introduction, she couldn't make herself go over and just talk with her. On top of it, she didn't know if the girl was interested in other girls. Sanja could end up looking foolish if she said something wrong. On the other hand, she didn't really have any friends, so would it really be so bad to strike a friendly conversation with another colleague? So what if nothing more came out of it? But even that thought wasn't enough for her to make any sort of a move. In the end, the insecurity won, and she stayed away from the other woman, keeping to herself at all times in the teachers lounge when both of them would be occupying it.

Except she never took into consideration that Ana could try and talk with her. So it would be foolish for this opportunity to pass.

Say something smart, she commanded herself. *Now.*

"Well, there is one creature in particular that interests me," she started, thinking of her roommate. "It's..."

"Ana, dear, sorry," the other Croatian teacher, an old woman close to retirement who couldn't stand the sight of Sanja, and vice versa, interrupted them. "There's a student right outside who needs to ask you something."

"Sorry," Ana apologized to Sanja, looking slightly disappointed, but it could've had something to do with a student nagging her during lunch break. "I need to see what this is about. Talk to you later."

And just like that, she went outside. Sanja wrestled with the need to burrow her head in her palms, unwilling to look pathetic amongst other teachers. Maybe it wouldn't last too long, maybe the student had some easy question that needed answering, and before long, Ana would be back and they would continue with their talk.

And Sanja would say to her what she was reading about, making it all sound very interesting and fun, not at all horrifying or as something that she's currently experiencing. And then maybe, just maybe, Ana would be hooked enough to ask her to continue their conversation after school and they'd go for a cup of coffee. She could almost see it to the point of tasting coffee on her tongue...

But it rang for the end of lunch break; the banging noise of a school bell burying her opportunity for interaction with Ana deeper in the grave. And she lost her chance. Again.

Sanja sighed and closed the book about impossible magical creatures whose whole purpose was to screw over human lives. There was a pressure on her shoulders and her steps were long and slow, but they somehow managed to bring her to the classroom, her personal Hell.

* * *

Paint, she commanded herself. The empty canvas was mocking her.

Sanja was sitting in front of it, cross legged. Acrylic paints were spread out before her, all of the colors that she'd bought months ago. Light yellow, burned brown and rusty red. The brush lay on the floor near her leg. She should start with picking it up.

Slowly, like there was a big weight bound at her arm, she managed to lower her hand and touch the brush. Gripping it proved even harder. But she managed to do that one simple thing, and even though her head made it seem like a slow motion sequence, it happened in a second, nothing more.

That was the first move. Now, she could paint. Now, she should paint.

The white of the canvas was a big offence. She tried to recollect the feeling she'd felt earlier in the day, while talking to Ana. That brief burst of energy that let the sun of Ana's smile touch her face, bathing her vision with warm colors. That moment when it looked like the girl was bigger than life; not just a substitute teacher, but a creature of nature, of beauty and life. She wanted to paint her there and then. But now nothing came. Whatever she'd felt, the afterthought of it lingered, but it stayed closed off from her, hiding behind the grey curtain in her mind. She couldn't bring it back. Instead, tiredness started to creep all over her, like an unwanted lover. The brush in her hand felt heavier than a ton.

From the corner of her eyes she could spot her old works, stacked against the wall. All of them were made during her time in college. There weren't many of them left, and she'd believed, once upon a time, she'll have more time when she's finally employed at a single place, instead of working multiple odd jobs to pay the rent while simultaneously being enrolled in college. And now she had the time, but no energy. She used to manage to do more when she was absolutely overwhelmed with assignments and minimum wage jobs, than she could do now.

Pathetic. Sanja sighed and put the brush down with effort. Her big plans for this room now seemed foolish. The previous owner was a teacher too, she'd learned, just like everyone else in the building given that it was commissioned by the teacher's association, like it was usual once upon a time in communist Yugoslavia. The woman whose apartment Sanja had bought didn't have any children of her own, so the room, whose purpose was probably to be a children's room, was turned into her home office. Like the rest of the flat, a lot of the original furniture and stuff had been left in here. Big wooden desk with drawers filled with old notebooks. Cabinets overflowing with old magazines and books.

The woman didn't have any close relations, no one who would take care of it, and some distant cousin who'd inherited the place had just put it on the market, without care for any of it. Or that was what they told Sanja. And without much thought she cleaned out the whole room. She'd sold the old books and magazines to the antique shops or put them into recycling, except for the few first issues of Croatian classics that she'd decided to keep for herself. She threw away all of the furniture with Shimun's help. She completely emptied out the whole room. She wanted to paint the walls in new colors, buy new pieces which would suit her needs more. But instead, she'd filled it with her old work and new supplies, but that was as far as she'd managed to go. And now, for months, it stayed like this. She threw out someone's entire life, and for what? Just so she could turn this room into a hollow skeleton of her dreams.

Her knees screamed at her for sitting in the same position for so long, but she couldn't find it in her to care. With her bone-weary eyes slowly closing, she finally decided that it was enough. The only thing she managed to do was torture herself. And she didn't need to do that, when there was a perfectly capable, unnatural entity living with her whose whole purpose was to do exactly that.

* * *

She managed to drag herself to the bed.

There was a brief debate held in her head whether there was any point in changing before sleep. She just wanted to lie in bed, retreat under the covers in her trousers and smelly t-shirt, but then remembered she wasn't technically alone. She was already looking like a loser, she didn't need to sink even lower in front of the creature haunting her. And with that thought she changed to pajamas before going to bed.

"I think I know what you are," she said to the empty room. She wondered what nightmare was waiting for her tonight. "I was doing some light reading today. Do you want to know what I learned?"

There was no answer.

"Okay. Be like that. I guess we will see each other soon enough."

* * *

There was a light breeze licking at her bare feet rooted in dirt scratching at her soles. The sky was so clear and blue, but she couldn't see the sun anywhere. It was so quiet that the absence of sound unnerved her, knowing fully well she should be able to hear the sea below, or the rustling of leaves behind her. There was nothing to hear, only shapes and colors to see.

She was standing at the edge of a precipice dressed in nothing but an old, vintage-looking nightie. It was full length, short sleeved, white, with a lace pattern over her chest and shoulders—but she couldn't remember ever owning something like that. Also, it didn't really fit her, as if it were borrowed, but who from or why she couldn't tell. Whoever it was, they were bigger than Sanja and the material kept blowing up in the wind, like a tent. Her long hair was let loose and it was dancing in the air just like her nightie, following music she couldn't hear, constantly getting into her eyes. It obscured a gut punch of a view—a huge, unstoppable sea, so dark grey against the blue sky that it looked black, stretching to eternity in front of her. There was something there, floating at the surface, but the fall was so long she couldn't discern what it was. Maybe if she just leaned over, she'd have a better view, but fear gripped her and she couldn't move. What if she lost balance and fell?

Sanja tried to get her legs to move backwards, to put some distance between herself and the edge, but they didn't work. Her feet were stuck to the rough ground, and no matter how much she tried, it was impossible for her to move them. Panic started gripping her heart. Something wasn't right, but the answer was constantly slipping from her mind.

A noise snuck upon her unprepared ears. She flinched in surprise. It was too low for her to understand what it was, but something told her it was nothing good, not with the way she couldn't move, the way her skin broke out in goosebumps and her heart started drumming faster. She was standing on the edge of the world and everything was either empty sky or dark sea or pure blankness of an undefined space behind her. There was nowhere to run.

She gripped the white fabric of the nightgown with her hands, trying to focus on the idea of walking, of movement. Ignoring the noise that had started rising, forming and shaping behind her back. She could recognise the sound of steps now, slowly coming closer. Approaching her without a hurry. Rhythmical. Mingled with another sound. Breathing... that wasn't hers. It belonged to the legs which could walk the ground unbound.

Sanja closed her eyes, silently pleading her body. It still refused to listen to her, as if she were made of fig bark and roots instead of blood and bones. The dark emptiness of her closed eyelids mocked her, amplifying the noises behind her back.

Painstakingly slowly, the steps continued their crescendo until Sanja could feel the presence close at her back. Will they continue? Would they walk until they're upon her immovable body? Her throat was completely dry and she hugged herself in anticipation.

The footsteps stopped. Someone was standing right behind her, close enough for her to feel the warm breath on the back of her neck. A single touch, burning through the fabric of her nightie, dropped on the low of her back, like a caress. She whimpered, but the sound disappeared in the wind that now gained momentum and started blowing stronger. The breathing came even closer to her skin, and she could feel the light touch of chapped lips against her earlobe.

"Do you know what I do to people like you?" Sanja heard the words whispered in her ear. Grandma's voice, distorted, but familiar. "I eat them alive."

The movement was so sudden Sanja didn't even have the time to register that she was in free fall before she hit the surface of the sea, hard.

Every bone in her body screamed in pain, like they'd broken in a thousand pieces upon impact. The oversized nightgown started twisting around her body, an unfortunate bondage, making it harder to move and almost impossible to swim in the sudden blurriness of underwater blue. Her hair was floating freely in front of her face, constantly getting in the way. It was becoming harder to think without air, as her lungs screamed for more. Instinct urged her to try moving upwards. Grasping through the water with her arms, she pushed, and pushed, forcing her body to move through the currents and the tangled mess of her gown, coming closer to the surface. Or at least what she hoped it was the right direction. Everywhere she looked she saw the same dark color, no sun which would shine upon her and show her the way.

Still, moving was better than drowning, so she swam and swam until she came face to face with a shape in the gloom—her own bloated face and dead, glassy eyes. The long hair on the corpse which was Sanja was like seaweed, its lips a color of an angry bruise. The dead, rotting Sanja reached out towards her, catching her arms with clammy hands. *Where are you going?* it seemed to be asking though nothing came out of its mouth. *This is our home now, stop fighting. Let it* eat *you before the sharks catch you. Before the world hunts you down and turns you into a soup.*

Sanja tried to get out of its grasp, but the drowned corpse's hands were iron strong. *It'll be better,* the dead her continued, *it'll be calm, safe.*

They floated together, almost embracing in the neverending dark blue, until finally, through tears, salt water and burning lungs, Sanja opened her mouth to a gurgled scream. The sea rushed through the opening, filling her up from the inside, leaving behind bubbles that escaped through her mouth.

There was no breath to be had, no fresh air, just the dead Sanja smiling with the bluish face of a fish caught in the dry land, right until darkness engulfed the living one, painting everything black.

3

Sanja woke up from the dream, gasping for breath like she was still underwater, her own choking breaths the only thing she could hear. There was an overbearing panic in her throat and she was unable to move, again, because there was something heavy pressing down on her chest. Squeezing her slowly, but unmistakably; crushing her lungs. She could imagine hearing her ribs shattering, breaking apart inside.

In the darkness of the room she could barely make out the outline of a dark shape and fiery red eyes. One of Sanja's arms was completely paralysed, but the other one felt free. Without much thought, she touched the mass that was pushing her down. Its texture was coarse, with muscles underneath, reminding her of a horse. It *felt* like a pony, squashing her to death with its weight. She would've probably laughed if she could breathe normally.

"Move," she managed to command through a gasp.

But the angry red eyes didn't listen to her. They just continued floating somewhere above her, presumably attached to a motionless head she couldn't see in the dark.

The weight was slowly crushing her into smithereens. *Was this another dream?* Was she dying? She couldn't move, couldn't breathe, could only lie frozen in darkness and in pain, drenched in sweat. But the thing had made a mistake, Sanja realized as she fought for air. It had tried to be creative with her nightmares, but in the manner of someone who knew only how to copy someone else's masterpiece, not create their own. She didn't need some dream dictionary to interpret her dreams nor resurrect Freud to explain its meaning. Grandma's voice, the fall, the pain, the dead Sanja in the sea—she knew what all of that was supposed to be. And it only made her furious.

She won't let herself be devoured.

"Move... or I swear I will slaughter you... and make myself... a nice, tasty meal... and fancy boots," she managed through ragged breath. "Even if... I had to do... that... as a ghost. I promise you." Speaking hurt but not as much as living in shame or the memory of death. Closing her free hand in fist, Sanja called on her remaining strength and managed to land a punch to the coarse body on her chest.

It wasn't a really strong hit. But the horse-like mass still disappeared into thin air.

Sanja gasped and inhaled air with the hunger of a person finally reaching the surface of the sea after they'd nearly drowned. And even though the sea belonged to her dream, Sanja was soaked through with sweat, so it really felt like her body had been submerged in water. Feeling slowly crawled back to her paralysed limbs, seeming at first like needles piercing her skin, bringing out even more pain. But this was a sweet one, since she knew it to mean she could move again.

Blinking sweat and tears from her eyes, Sanja focused on her surroundings. She was alone in the bed... but there was something watching her from the darkness. The intensity of the gaze fell upon Sanja's exposed skin and she hated it.

She sat up in bed and switched the bedside lamp on with shaking hands. Light hurt her eyes, temporarily blinding her, but she opened them again not long after and took in the sight before her. The old wooden wardrobe across her queen size bed. The nightstand on her right—holding a lamp, the book about supernatural creatures from Učka, and a plate with old, uneaten muffins. A chair covered in already worn clothes by the bed, next to it a small pile of Sanja's discarded socks on the floor and, in the middle of them, a strange woman with black hair in a vintage-looking white dress.

She didn't expect it to look like a Goth.

The woman was watching her silently, without blinking, holding herself so still that not an inch of her body nor her long white dress was moving. Like a figure in the photograph made alive. Sanja sat frozen for a moment, concentrating on her own loud breaths resounding in the room; something to celebrate. There were no sounds of breathing coming from the other person, though.

That was a chilling thought. Something she didn't really want to ponder.

The lack of noise was starting to get on Sanja's nerves, reminding her too much of the dream, that feeling of unstoppable asphyxiation still fresh inside her mind. Now, her own breathing felt heavy, intense. Like Sanja's lungs hurt just from watching the mora's unmoving chest.

Nothing was happening, and it was somehow worse than any alternatives she could imagine. What was it with this waiting, which made it scarier than the other woman actually doing something? Maybe she was just waiting for Sanja to fall back to sleep, where she could continue to do to her whatever she wanted to.

Sanja couldn't stand this anymore, there had to be something she could do, something she could say to diminish this suffocating presence. "Well, that was bad," she settled on. "Did you really just try to kill me? Or was this merely a part of the act?"

But the woman didn't answer. She just creepily stood near Sanja's bed, her feet hidden in Sanja's worn, stinky socks, watching her without blinking, or breathing, or twitching; still as a tombstone in the middle of a graveyard.

"I know what you are," Sanja continued, indicating the book on her nightstand with the slight movement of her head. "You're the *mora*, aren't you?" Not just any nightmare, but *the* nightmare. One of the creatures appearing in the form of a woman whose whole purpose was to bring night terrors, while strangling the dreamer and sucking out their life energy. And yet, giving it a name didn't change a thing in their interaction. The woman just stood there, eyes unblinking, drinking in the sight of a disheveled Sanja as if it were the most interesting thing in the world. What the hell was she planning?

"You know what, you're boring me," Sanja said in the end, since it had become apparent that the mora didn't plan on saying or doing anything. If she reduced her to a joke, a bad dream that meant nothing in the day, maybe she could banish her away.

"Always the same with the nightmares. It's irritating. But I can be irritating as well. The way I see it, you're the one who's stuck here with me. So *I'm* going to haunt *you*. With... with..." For a moment she wasn't certain that her brain was working as it should be. But the more she looked at the source of her nightmares, the angrier she got, still feeling the burn on her chest. There was probably nothing she could do to make it hurt, and if there was a way to kill the creature it wasn't written in the book. But she refused to be some damsel quaking in fear on her own bed. If she wanted to live like that she would've stayed with her Grandma and not be obligated to the bank for a big chunk of her life. And she would rather let the Goth woman eat her alive before uttering a word of Christian prayer, even though she knew it worked. Letting her dear cousin read from the damned Bible was one thing, but saying any of the prayers Grandma taught her aloud was another.

And then she got an idea. "I'm going to haunt you with the methods of teaching literature as a part of Croatian Language in primary schools. Let's start with the purpose of teaching literature," she lifted one finger. "Firstly, it helps to develop reading comprehension—which is very important, because kids use spoken and written language to learn other subjects. Secondly," another finger was lifted, "it develops their creativity and literary capabilities, not to mention cultivating their interest in our cultural heritage and enriching their spirit."

The woman finally blinked; the first movement she made ever since appearing before Sanja. Following it was a look Sanja could only describe as uttermost confusement, making her think this sort of thing never happened to the mora, and now she didn't know how to react. Or she was simply shocked that someone would try a tactic this dumb. Whatever was the case, Sanja smirked, relishing in thought that she was making an evil entity uncomfortable with her work talk.

Wanting to up the ante, she got out of bed and walked to the living room. The woman followed, gliding through the air, her brows slightly lowered and her nose scrunched as if smelling something much worse than Sanja's sleeping sweat and old socks. Probably the two weeks' worth of trash that was still piling under the sink.

Sanja found what she was looking for on her bookshelf; the big, hardcover red book that she opened on random. "Curriculum theory, perfect, let's read about that, shall we?"

She sat down on the couch and read aloud, completely tuning out from the actual meaning of the text. The words kept coming with the rhythm of her breaths, while the presence lingered at her back. Sanja kept reading, calming down with each new chapter, words slowly slurring with time, keeping it up even after the woman had disappeared, well in the night.

Until she finally managed to fall asleep again, completely exhausted, right there on the couch; this time without nightmares—for now.

* * *

Life really hated Sanja. Or, maybe it was her strange roommate pulling the strings behind the curtains, if it were even capable of something like that. Probably wasn't, but it was easier to blame someone else for her shitty day. The mora was conspicuously missing from her dreams so Sanja has blessedly not dreamt about anything at all for a whole week. But just because there were no nightmares, or farm animals crushing her chest when she woke, it didn't mean that everything was fine. It categorically wasn't.

First, she was almost late for class because everyone seems to forget how to drive when it's raining, nevermind that it's almost always raining in Rijeka, which is kind of convenient given that the town name, quite literally, meant *river*. Then, her pupils were especially difficult. Maybe they didn't talk loudly and fight among themselves, or throw stuff across the classroom, or carve their names and curses with their scissors into the desk surfaces, but they were definitely sleeping awake, instead of listening to the exciting tale of a shoemaker trying to outwit the devil. Even those ambitious few who usually had the willpower to learn and a love of reading didn't have any concentration at all, completely drained of any emotion or resolve. They made her sleepy too, in return, ready to sit at her desk and take a nap. And wouldn't it be something to see? Especially if the mora had followed her to the school...

To make things worse, after the class, one angry parent appeared at the teacher's lounge door, looking for Sanja, ready to fight. Because, obviously, she was the one to blame that the son was unprepared for the exam. Sanja spent three quarters of an hour listening to this woman throwing all sorts of thinly veiled insults into her face, while *she*, as a teacher, had to stay perfectly calm and professional. Even though all she wanted to do was just *hit* the woman with her school planner, hard, continuously, until she stopped talking, until there were teeth, knocked out from her jaw, all over the floor.

Sanja gripped the planner, but didn't move, patiently waiting for the woman to leave.

Also, she still wasn't sure where she stood with Ana. The young woman continued throwing smiles and glances her way in the teacher's lounge, even coming over to Sanja's seat a few times to chat about books and work, gossip about students and their parents—but Sanja still didn't know what to make of her. Was she interested in Sanja as a colleague, a possible friend or, if she dared to hope, something more romantic? And would Sanja be brave enough to try and do something, if that was the case?

As a cherry on the top of it all, interrupting her well earned peaceful afternoon, her other cousin Marija suddenly showed up at Sanja's door with her son in tow. The knocking found her just when she was slicing through a Sachertorte she'd planned on eating instead of lunch.

"Really, it's this teacher's fault, he doesn't know how to teach and Dario is really trying—but how could he succeed on his own when he doesn't understand a thing?" Marija was talking with her mouth full of the store bought chocolatey goodness, but Sanja wasn't really listening to a word she was saying. They used to be close, once upon a time. Not as Sanja and Shimun, though—Marija's mom never let her daughter spend the summers with Grandma, a sore point in their family. The older Sanja got, it was easier to understand her Aunt. Marija also found Sanja a bit weird, not something that she'd ever say out loud, of course, but Sanja could feel that in every uncertain smile Marija ever threw her way. It was a bit harder to connect with her, but they were still friends.

But whatever they'd had as kids just wasn't there anymore, slowly melting away ever since Marija's teenage pregnancy and shotgun wedding. Different paths in life tend to do that to relationships. Especially when children were involved.

"Hmmm? Oh, yeah, yeah, you're right," Sanja mumbled through a mouthful of Sachertorte which tasted like disappointment and unfulfilled plans, not really aware of what she was agreeing with right now. She'd bought it chasing sweet serotonin, wanting to come home and devour it without any sense or sensibility, sitting at the countertop, alone, contemplating her life choices, with a glass of Teacher's whisky for her teacher's life. She did also plan, briefly, to try and google moras and such, her book proving too theoretic after all. Unsurprising, since it wasn't really intended to be a guide for banishing supernatural creatures, not even for believing in them—but it was still disappointing.

"It's, it's, you know, a mess. This whole country and our schools, I mean, do you know how many textbooks they have? And how much homework? It's not normal! And I tried to help him with these, these Paul boys..."

"The Paul Street Boys," Sanja offered.

"Yeah, but he really doesn't understand a thing..." *Don't lie, he didn't even try reading it*, Sanja thought, knowing Marija's son. "And I tried to read it and help him..." *you wanted to write it instead of him, so he doesn't get bad grades, God forbid*, "but I don't understand it myself. It's so hard!" *Yeah, it's really a confusing piece of text, this story of bullying and kid's play going too far, truly on par with James Joyce's Ulysses*, Sanja wanted to say, but decided to keep it to herself.

She looked at Dario—the kid in question—who was sitting on the couch playing on his smartphone, several generations better than Sanja's. He was a burly boy with brown hair best described as boring, shared by all of the family, dressed in fancy designer clothes, probably more expensive than all of Sanja's wardrobe combined, with an air of superiority that could compete with that of a politician. He'd barely greeted Sanja before sitting down on her couch and losing himself in a mind numbing game. But who was she to judge him? His mother and Sanja weren't just grownups, they were also his family, which made them as interesting to watch as a two hour documentary about photosynthesis.

"So I thought, you know, *our Sanja could help*. It's her job to explain these things to kids."

"Of course." She got up from the dining table and went to get the wine. Marija was sipping her overly sweetened white coffee but Sanja needed something stronger. Whisky would be better, and she sadly glanced at the Teacher's on her great wooden shelf, but it wasn't appropriate in this sort of a situation. That, and the last thing she needed was her cousin spreading news to the rest of the family how she was becoming an alcoholic. "I could help him, explain it to him, but I won't write it for him. You know, his teacher would totally know if the paper was written by another teacher. It's a thing. We know," she told Marija from the kitchen. Squashy sounds of something dropping down emanated from Dario's phone, drilling a brand new headache in her brain. It was the only thing he contributed to their conversation, like a language he knew but the adults didn't speak.

"Of course, of course. I wouldn't ask something like that of you." Lies. Marija had planned on doing just that, and her forced smile betrayed both her thoughts and her disappointment.

Sanja took a corkscrew out of the drawer. The thought of stabbing her arm and making a vertical slash flashed in her mind, making her wonder what it would feel like. How would her cousin react to see Sanja's veins opened up? Her tongue felt dry and swollen, and she discarded the fleeting visual of hot red blood dropping on the grey marble floor, focusing on the *now*.

"Dario, come here. Let's see those questions you have. Marija, some wine? I know you're driving, but a glass won't hurt." Her voice was pitched too high, but she hoped her cousin wouldn't notice anything amiss. Marija nodded, but *drop*, *splash*, *squash* and *ping* were the only answers Dario had to offer.

"Dario, sweetie, come here. Didn't you hear what your aunt said?"

"No," he answered, not moving his eyes from the phone. "One more minute."

Marija shrugged, shrouded in a purple cloud of shame. It was an ugly thing, like a bruise on her face. Sanja saw Marija in all her helplessness, sitting with her mousy hair falling down like a dead animal's pelt; the lines on her face a web of regret. She was two years younger than Sanja, had no job, but lived in luxury thanks to her husband's seafaring paychecks, wearing expensive clothes and perfumes, going to manicures and pedicures and all those skin care routines Sanja couldn't even name... and yet, at that moment Marija looked older than her. Subdued, more exhausted, and so worn out that Sanja could feel nothing but bad for her.

Marija's fingers accepted a tall glass of wine like a small blessing. If Sanja could draw right now, she would portray Marija with white, thin fish bones on the table in front of her, a few even protruding from the skin of her arms, and a necklace made of sharp rocks around her neck, anchoring her to the floor.

"Dario, come here, right now! We're not going to waste your aunt's time. Games can wait."

"I said," he looked at them like he was looking at a pair of particularly annoying mosquitos, "one more minute." The game emitted a shrill sound and Dario squealed like a lamb brought to slaughter. "Look what you did! I've made a mistake! This will cost me my ranking!"

"Great, that means you can come now and do your reading assignment," his mother said. "You don't want another F."

"I don't care! It's a stupid book! Why can't she explain it to you, and then you can tell me about it at home?"

Marija looked at Sanja, obviously wondering if they could do exactly that. Sanja honestly didn't care either way, she just wanted to be left alone with her cake.

A sudden sensation brushed across her back, the feeling of someone walking right behind her, approaching them. She sat up ramrod straight, goosebumps breaking out on the skin of her arms. Something soft and warm, with the definite feeling of a body, touched her legs lightly. She forced herself not to react. Of all days, her roommate had to choose today to show herself. If Marija learned of Sanja's terrible haunting, it won't be long until Grandma hears about it herself, and then Sanja would have a completely new nightmare to live in.

"Oh!" Marija exclaimed, watching the floor near Sanja's chair, making her insides churn, "I didn't know you had a cat!"

The statement was so unexpected, Sanja almost fell from her chair.

'I didn't either' wasn't a very promising answer, so Sanja swallowed it and followed Marija's gaze. And there she was, a black cat with a small tuft of white fur under her neck. Sanja wondered if the mora was imitating E. A. Poe on purpose, if she even knew about the man and his stories. Or—and here was an interesting thought—if Poe had also had an experience with the supernatural. Maybe he had his own mora haunting his dreams, slowly torturing him to an early grave. The cat meowed, as if mocking her, and then showed both women she butt with a fluffy tail raised high. She went straight to Dario, who looked at her with disdain before returning to his game.

Briefly wondering if she should intervene, Sanja found that she was morbidly curious about what would happen next. This was the first time the mora manifested in the light of day, and in front of others no less. She'd read in the book that it could take the form of a feline, of course, but she wasn't expecting it to happen while she was having guests. Her ideas had run more along the line of waking up one night from a nightmare with a cat on her chest, clawing her eyes out.

"Anyway, I have the list of questions here," Sanja heard her cousin say, followed by the rustling of a hand going through the contents of a bag. The cat was still meowing and brushing against Dario's leg, even though he was doing his best to ignore her. He finally jerked his leg trying to get the cat to move away, but she just jumped on the couch close to him, unperturbed.

"Go away, you stupid cat. You'll leave your hair everywhere." The boy tried to knock the animal down from the couch, and Sanja saw it in slow motion. The cat, jumping into the air, catching the boy's hand with its claws, and biting hard.

"Ow! Fucking cat!" he shrieked as the cat continued hanging from his arm, until he managed to shrug her off, cursing loudly. It was weirdly satisfying and humorous to see that, even though Sanja wasn't sure why she enjoyed looking at the boy's discomfort that much. It wasn't right. And yet... the cat licked the blood off its muzzle, its bright eyes directly at Sanja, like she wanted to say—*more, more of this, please*. Like Sanja could understand that need.

"Language, Dario!" his mother scolded him. "Oh, poor baby. Your cat is a beast, Sanja," Marija said, observing her son's hand like a hawk, while the cat wrinkled her little whiskers. Sanja came closer to inspect the wound, but even though the mora had drawn blood it looked shallow, like nothing to be worried about. It was almost disappointingly anticlimactic, like a part of her wanted even more drama, even more blood.

"Well, you know cats. They like to show their affection by biting." The cat looked at her like she was personally offended with what Sanja had said, before she padded off somewhere in the direction of the bedroom, or, just as easily, vanishing as soon as she was out of sight. Sanja didn't care to check, choosing to take one last bite from the cake instead, feeling the sweet chocolate melting on her tongue, knowing fully well she probably won't be able to get a good night's rest tonight no matter what she did. She briefly wondered if she should try to stay awake all night, just in case, like she used to do when she was younger. But she had a job now and if she wanted to keep it and get paid for it, she needed to be able to function in the morning.

"It's going to be alright," she heard Marija coddle her son like he was recovering from an attack by some wild beast, not something that looked like a domestic cat. "But honestly, Sanja, you should discipline that pet. It's dangerous."

Sanja shrugged and sipped on her wine. "It's just a cat, it's what they do," Sanja didn't have to defend her fake cat, but found it amusing. This was the first thing in this, very depressing day, that made her chuckle inside. Even though it will probably end in her tears. It was good that she found something funny about her situation, or her life would end up looking even gloomier than it already did.

"And that's why dogs are better," Marija concluded. Dario had already gone back to his game, apparently not that traumatised with the vicious attack. Sanja wondered if there were going to be consequences for him, if he'll be haunted too. A good person would warn them, or try to stop the mora before getting into contact with a kid, but instead, Sanja stayed and let things play out, not bothering to intervene. She was a bad person, surely. After everything her Grandma did to make her grow up a saint, it looked like she was going straight to Hell.

It wasn't that surprising, given that Grandma made it abundantly clear that there was no room in Heaven for lesbians.

Sanja swallowed up the bite of her Sachertorte, enjoying the taste of apricot jam and said: "Let's look at those questions. You don't want to stay here too late. And it will soon be dark."

* * *

It was calm below the old mulberry tree, her favorite spot in her grandmother's garden. The leaves softly crackled with the wind and the grass rustled as if a snake were moving through it. Dry, sandy soil felt rough where she was lying down on her back. The familiarity made her smile.

Sanja used to play in that particular sandy spot when she was a child. Drawing in sand, getting herself dusty and dirty, always to the point of earning a whipping for ruining her clothes. This was also the place where she'd first encountered a supernatural being—a ghost. The memory was blurry and vague, an impression rather than a narrative; Sanja having sticky fingers, happily playing alone until a sudden presence of a kind old man interrupted her. He took her in his arms, lifting her up from the ground, and his embrace was gentle and warm and full of love, unlike anything else she felt. It disappeared when Grandma came out of the house. Without the man holding her, there was only the air and gravity that brought Sanja hard on the land. She scraped her knees so hard the scars were still there even to this day. Years later, Grandma finally admitted that it was her deceased husband, foaming at the mouth at the idea that he came to see his granddaughter and not her.

Something small and sticky fell down on Sanja's forehead, bringing her to the present. She opened her eyes and removed it with her hand, her fingers coming away bloodred. *Just a mulberry fruit, then.* But when she licked it, the taste was wrong—bitter metal, rotten, devoid of sweetness. She frowned and looked up at the thick canopy, where dark purple, almost black mulberries pulsed in the sun, oozing with blood. Tiny drops were raining on her forehead, her hair and even in her eyes, bathing her in red. She wiped away the juice from her eyes like tears, when the soft hissing sound near her legs startled her.

There, in the large, dense fig shrub—which her grandma grew for marmalade—something was moving. Sanja rose from the ground, barefoot, feeling the rough sand between her toes. Who knew what kind of creepy crawlies were in the grass or how many thorn branches hiding beneath the shrubbery. But, whatever had made the noise had started to move away, and she wanted, no, *needed* to know what it was. Sanja found not knowing annoying, like a word on the tip of the tongue that kept getting away.

She found the strength to follow the sound, crawling under the shrub.

Sharp, meaty fig leaves scratched all over her body, leaving her skin irritated. They blocked the sunshine and slowly turned into a tunnel that brought her to an old house. It should have been her Grandma's childhood home, where they used to spend their summer days, but it looked all wrong. For starters, it was in the wrong place. Behind the fig tree, there was usually a big green field with a small vineyard, and the house was supposed to be at the opposite side, behind Sanja's back. Instead, it was in front of her, waiting, calling to her, its huge wooden doors slightly ajar.

It was made of stone, grey and monumental, too big—at the same time, Grandma's old house and not. As if her brain was having difficulties remembering the right place, conjuring something new in its stead. Pulled by some invisible force, she knew she had to get inside.

The doors opened to a huge empty space, a hearth in its middle, one they definitely didn't have when she was a kid. Dried herbs that she couldn't name were hanging all over the place, the air heavy with the scent of a spicy stew. Her eyes were drawn to the table in the corner, with dried figs laid on a white tablecloth, just like Grandma used to do. But it wasn't the figs that got her attention—the privilege belonged to a slim walnut branch set innocently in the middle of them. Cut from a tree and devoid of leaves, the branch was flexible in a way which made it perfect for a homemade whip. It could even make a distinct cracking sound during the lashing, always loud in Sanja's ears as the branch sailed through the air before settling on her back. Her skin prickled with phantom flashes. The promise of hot, searing pain was written all over the long walnut body. Sanja's throat constricted.

Quiet sucking sounds distracted her and she finally managed to turn her gaze away from the cane. It couldn't do anything to her, but she still knew exactly where it was in relation to her, while the sound drew her to a big, closed metal door in the back. She knew what was expected of her. To put her hand against its cold surface, to grip the doorknob and open it. But just because that was the way the story ended, she didn't want to do it. Didn't want to find out what made that horrible suckling noise, reminding her of people gnawing at bones or slurping up shrimps. There were a lot of surprises which could be waiting for her inside, and most of them probably wouldn't be good at all. It could be her Grandma, to begin with, in the middle of her meal, and then the whip would finally serve its purpose. And now the sound—like it knew she feared it—became louder; this time unmistakably the noise of someone eating behind the doors.

Her hand moved on her own, grasping the doorknob against her better judgement. Fear rose from her stomach to her throat like acid, her body ready to throw up. She screamed internally to turn around and go back, but her mind betrayed her and she opened the door.

To a sight so repugnant and utterly unexpected but, somehow, not that strange to her. On a small bed lay her cousin's son Dario, sleeping, like the innocent angel people believed children to be. Kneeling beside him was the mora, sucking on his barefoot toes, like it was pork. She engulfed his big toe in her mouth, her eyes closed in delight. Sanja must've made a sound of disgust or something because the other woman opened her eyes and caught Sanja's gaze, her black pupils expanding in surprise. She spat out the kid's toe with a loud wet sound and the expression of a cat caught with stolen slices of ham.

"Please," the mora said in raspy, low sounds of rats confined within walls. Sanja stood numb, shocked more because it was the first time she'd heard the woman speak, than because of what she was witnessing. "I'm hungry. Please. Find someone who tastes better. This one's bitter and sour. But I'm so, so hungry, I'll eat anything. Even him. If I may. Please."

Sanja opened her mouth to answer, even though she wasn't sure what she'd say, but suddenly she was awake, and all alone, in her queen-size bed.

4

Eighth graders were in an especially hellish mood today. It wasn't an unusual sort of behavior for this group, famous throughout the school for their problematic and disrespectful behaviour, but it looked like it was going to be one of those days when they were truly intolerable.

After her last dream, Sanja spent the night over a book, her eyelids huge and weighting down, but she refused to close them. Given the fact she didn't have a good night's sleep—with the image of her relative's kid toes getting sucked by an ancient nightmare entity haunting her to the point she was afraid to close her eyes again—she got to her class annoyed, tired and nursing a headache. Meaning, she had even less tolerance for the students' behavior then usual.

"Ivan, please sit down right now!" she yelled, her voice fighting with the others shouting in the classroom.

"I did," the student smirked from where he was sitting on the desk.

"In your place!"

"Sure," he said and put his leg up on another student's chair.

"Professor!" that student wailed. "Ivan put his leg on my chair!"

"I can see that, Lovro."

A couple of kids sniggered from the back, watching the situation unfold.

"SIT DOWN!" Her voice boomed all over the place like a banshee's cry.

Ivan finally, albeit slowly, moved to his chair.

"Now, what do you think one can find in biographies? What sort of information?"

Ivan turned around and started playing with the kids in the next row. She closed her eyes for a moment before opening them again. A student sitting in the first row raised his arm with an honest to god answer. And a good one too. Sanja turned to write it down on the blackboard, talking all the time with the front row student, but watching all of them.

Two distinctive groups slowly formed. One around Ivan, and the other among the girls on Sanja's left. Boys played one of their new games, the one where they literally kept hitting each other, and one kid had his eyes closed, trying to guess who in the group had hit him. The girls loudly talked to each other and one of them pulled out a comb, of all things, and started doing other girls' hair.

Sanja found herself frozen in the moment. What could she do? Yelling didn't work, she could lose her voice, and it would be pointless. She could complain to the class' homeroom teacher, but her colleague couldn't do anything smart anyway, except talk to their parents, which she had already done, and it didn't work. She could write them up, pages upon pages detailing their unacceptable behavior—and for what? Hold an impromptu exam right now, five minutes for each kid? They would all get an F and go straight back to whatever they were doing right now, and *she* was the one that would have to deal with their abysmal grades later. She felt completely hopeless and helpless, and it was draining her of all her willpower.

And with her strength drained, the whole world suddenly went grey, saturation turning down. Sanja's stomach rumbled with the force of a storm closing in from the sky. The hunger crept inside of her; ice dead fingers piercing her abdomen. Small wonder, really, given that she couldn't remember the last time she ate. There was the chocolate cake, the taste just a memory, from yesterday. After that, it was only a cup of scorching coffee, taken in the morning rush to get to her job on time.

Children looked at her, their faces confused, fleshy and pink, their bodies full of meat and fat.

I could bring them home, feed them to the woman. Sanja's mouth watered, thinking of getting food. Did the mora feel like that all the time? Emptiness gnawing at her insides, just a huge, unfulfilled pit waiting for scraps? The woman was so hungry, she'd outright pleaded for food. And who was Sanja to deny her that? She could herd them like the sheep they were and leave them at the mora's mercy; let her suck their bones clean.

Her own belly hurt, empty apart from digesting coffee, now turned to acid that burns through her stomach tissue. Oh how sweet would it be, to taste the sweet, greasy steak, sliced from the children's muscle fibers, melting on her tongue. Seeing the blood seeping on the grill, letting it cook until just raw, so the metallic taste stays. Or, she could boil their little arms and legs, season them with rosemary, basil and parsley, until it's buttery soft under her teeth, easy to suck the bones dry...

It would be so easy to just collect them, take them by their soft little arms, bring their meaty bodies to her flat, leave them to the mora and the sharpened knives waiting ready in the kitchen drawer. To cut out and carve, to slice and chop, until nothing is left except dark red food, neatly labeled in the fridge.

Silence would be so sweet. She wouldn't have a perpetual headache. She could draw again, her stomach full, her arms light.

The urge to gather them all like ducks for Christmas dinner was so strong it washed over her sight and painted the world red.

“Teacher?” It was the student from the front. The word jerked Sanja from her thoughts and the cold fingers which were holding her tight abruptly let go of her lungs. Her palm hurt, crescent imprints of her nails left all over the flesh. She could still envision claws tearing meat from the bones. Swallowing the bitter saliva down, she forced her thoughts to disperse, like a shroud blown away on the wind.

“Yes, Leo?” she asked, shaken up. Without the visions of blood, the only thing left were hunger and fear for her mental state. And the never ending headache pounding in her head, like a bad metal band’s drums.

“How do we know if the information in a biography is correct and not invented by the author?” Leo asked.

Sanja blinked, founding her footing in the present. The table and the blackboard came into focus again. She looked at the curious pupil all over as he patiently waited for an answer, and then the other kids. Most of them still weren’t paying attention.

But so what? Smirking Ivan’s dad was in all certainty probably beating him, but no one could do anything about it. Social services were completely useless. Two of the boys playing alongside Ivan had serious learning impairments, and they should’ve had an assistant each, working individually with them all the time. The school lacked funds for a teacher’s assistant. Without one, alone in her classroom, it was impossible to help them and adhere to the yearly plan Sanja was supposed to see through. The girls in the other group all lived with different sorts of neglect at home and just needed some attention. It wasn’t strange that the whole class was a mess. ‘Special care department’, some of the teachers said in hushed tones, except no one was giving them any of the special care they desperately needed. No one had time for that. Not with their weekly plans and programs and administrative tasks.

And now... how could she think about offering them to the mora, just because they were annoying? Having those horrible thoughts in her head, something must’ve definitely been wrong with her. *It was the mora. She did something to me. She's still with me*, Sanja frantically thought, forcing herself to calm down. *Maybe I'm still dreaming*.

But she wasn't. She was fairly sure of that. Even though nothing was certain anymore, and the reality looked as unreal as the dreams, while the dreams looked as real as her breathing.

And that thought frightened her.

She turned back to the student in the front row, who now looked concerned.

"That's a very good question, Leo," she commended him with shaky breath, and got back to work, ignoring the lump-like heaviness in her breasts.

* * *

Sanja rushed through packing her things, wanting to disappear from the teacher's lounge before another colleague started talking to her, or the headmistress asked her to substitute for someone who'd ended up unexpectedly absent from work. The taste of bleakness still clung to her, and she desperately needed to clear her head, as far away from the school as possible. The last thing she needed was to become a headline in the crime pages, to completely lose touch with reality and end up as some sort of cannibalistic serial killer. Grandma would get an instant heart attack if that happened. Well, when she put things like that, maybe it would be worth it...

"Hey, done for today?" Ana materialized behind her back while Sanja was putting on her leather jacket, making her jump out of her own skin and lose the jacket on the floor. "Sorry, did I scare you?" she asked, with a confused smile, her eyes twinkling like bonfire embers dancing in the night.

Sanja knew she must have looked spooked, so she tried to put on the most reassuring smile she could find. “Oh! Oh, no, I was just lost in thoughts. But yeah, I’m done and I’m totally exhausted. Just... waiting to get home... to my cat.” She cringed inwardly. She tried so hard not to sound pathetic, to look like a normal human being who had something more in her life then just an empty apartment, that it was no wonder she ended up saying the stupidest thing she could think of. Her cat. Hah!

“Oh, you have a cat! That’s so cool, I always wanted to have one, but my parents hate them, so we got a dog.”

A slight redness coloured Ana’s cheeks; probably because she was embarrassed at having to still live with her parents. Sanja could understand that. If you didn’t have a steady job, but kept substituting after college, or if you didn’t have a life partner to pick up the bills in the jobless periods... wait, that meant Ana wasn’t living with a boyfriend, like most of the young teachers Sanja knew, and at least that was promising! Still—it didn’t mean a thing, not really. No, really.

“What kind is it? Your cat?”

“Er... a... black. European domestic cat. You know. The normal one.”

“And what’s its name? Our dog’s Rex. I know, I know, not really an original one...”

“...Poe.” This conversation was getting out of hand. Now her not-cat had a name. And she was still in the school building, and the probability of having to stay and substitute for someone was growing exponentially. But it was nice, just talking to Ana. Even her headache started to ease up a bit.

“Because it’s black? Or because you teach literature and there is a little bit of an old school, pretentious teacher in you?”

“If that were the case I would call it something like... Shenoa.” Ana burst into laughter, like Sanja had told a joke worthy of stand up comedy. It wasn’t that funny, was it?

But then again, there wasn't a person alive who'd gone to a Croatian school who wasn't traumatised with the guy who wrote the first Croatian novel and ended being canonized no matter how boring it was, so maybe it was funny, after all, in a sort of sad and pathetic way.

"Hey, so I still have two classes for today, and I only have a minute, but we need to go grab a cup of coffee one day, don't you think? When do we have a break together? If you have time, of course. I'm only here for a couple of days more," Ana said, as if Sanja could've somehow missed the fact.

Sanja was suddenly acutely aware that they weren't alone in the teacher's lounge and that the faculty nun was standing by the copier. She was minding her own business, though, probably printing materials for her Bible study class, and Sanja needed to relax. After all, the question was innocent enough. Going to coffee was a normal thing for any Croatian—there was even an article how it was a part of Croatian culture, that they'd laughed about once in the lounge—and it wasn't even like it would be the first time she went for coffee on a break. She did it a few times with some of the younger English teachers. It was a normal question. No one would think of it otherwise.

Still, a heavy blanket of fear descended on her vision, making the world tilt a bit. The rhythmic machine noise was a constant in her ears, reminding her that the nun was still working the copier. Sanja needed to calm down before she broke out in sweat and rugged breaths.

"Yeah, yeah, sure." She tried to look as normal as possible. Nothing to see here, sister Veronika.

"Cool! Oh, the bell! Need to go, see you soon!" Ana flashed her a big grin and waved before disappearing outside the lounge.

Sanja buttoned up her jacket and mumbled goodbye to sister Veronika before rapidly making her escape, too. She ran away from the building as if it were a crime scene she was responsible for, but managed to slow down eventually to avoid looking like an axe wielding maniac. As she did, she realized she was fighting a small smile breaking on her face, almost forgetting for a moment the thoughts clouding her brain during her last class.

* * *

The internet was completely useless—even less helpful than her book on Croatian folk tales—like it usually gets when one has to deal with Croatian matters. Googling the mora ended up a pointless task. The few sentences on the Croatian Wikipedia didn't expand much with the English translation. The other search results were mostly about unconnected, similarly spelled words, or *Kikimoras*, which could be the Polish version of the mora—or something from a fantasy series, she wasn't too sure. It also didn't help that the English Wikipedia entry on moras tried to convince her that Polish people protected themselves from a mora either by drinking coffee before sleep—which would probably mean no sleeping, no wonder it could help, but being constantly exhausted couldn't be feasible in long term—or by smearing feces on the front door. Which, just. No. The thought of her neighbours' faces if she'd do that made her close up the laptop in frustration.

Disappointing, but not surprising. Why couldn't she deal with some of the supernatural creatures Grandma told her about? Take ghosts, for example. She knew how to handle ghosts. Just light a candle for them and they'll go away, seeing they were appreciated. Or werewolves. Grandma talked about how, when she was a kid, one of the village men turned up to be the werewolf slaughtering their sheep during the night. Some of the villagers hunted him down while he was turned, put him in a bag, and beat the shit out of him, leaving him bound in the bag until the morning. When the sun came, they opened it and saw which one of them was a shapeshifter. After that he couldn't attack the sheep anymore, knowing the other men could come to his house at any time.

But no, she had to deal with a mora, whose whole purpose was to torment her with asphyxiating nightmares. Which ended with people online coming to a natural conclusion that if you didn't want to deal with the mora's terrors, you simply shouldn't fall asleep.

The doorbell rang, making her recoil in surprise. She wasn't expecting anyone, and it was almost evening. The slight touch of panic gripped her—making her wonder if it was a serial killer, a rapist or a neighbour—and she contemplated not opening at all, acting like she wasn't at home.

"Sanja, it's me. Are you in there?"

She finally exhaled the air she kept in, groaning out loud. She should contemplate the feces-on-door-frame protection, maybe Polish were getting somewhere with that.

Shimun's face at the doors made her careful not to roll her eyes. Relatives. They never knew how to pick up the phone and ask if it was alright to drop by. Or was it just a priest thing? Except Marija did that too... so no, it was probably in their blood.

"Dearest cousin of mine, what brings you to my completely normal and humble abode?"

He didn't laugh, of course, Sanja didn't expect him to. Shimun gave her a new bottle of wine, at least, and got in the flat, unamused. "I've talked to Marija..."

"Oh, did you?" She closed the doors behind him, eyeing the bottle. Not altar wine this time. It was for the better; she wasn't certain she could stomach it again.

"Yes, and she mentioned your cat. How interesting. I didn't know you had a cat," the disappointment dripped from his voice, mixed with a teaspoon of sadness. Was it because he thought she didn't tell him about getting a pet, or because he knew it had to be her supernatural problem?

"Got it after your last visit, cuz," she said jokingly, but then heard a hissing sound. And there it was, the damn cat, when she wasn't there before; standing on the windowsill, her black fur electrified in tall little spikes, showing her teeth to Shimun and protesting his appearance. Speak of the devil...

"Careful, she bites," Sanja said through a sigh. Of course the mora would choose this moment to materialise. Sanja hadn't seen her since the last dream, and a part of her was dreading her return, not because of what the mora could do to her, but because of what *Sanja* would want to do to someone else. Since she was still not over the incident at school, uncertain whether her thoughts were influenced by the mora or if she was slowly losing her mind, that fear lingered somewhere in the background, but she also felt too tired to worry about it *too* much. She just buried it deep inside, like everything else.

"Is this a *cat* cat, or..." he left his question hanging in the air, appearing momentarily confused. Sanja didn't answer, but poured them both some wine instead, feeling a sort of déjà vu. It was white this time, though. The cat in question looked at Shimun with pure hatred in her glassy eyes. "It's not," he came to the conclusion in the end, and made a sign of the cross in the air. It only made the hissing and meowing angrier, as if she was ready to start pounding him.

"Shut up, both of you," Sanja said tiredly, not wanting any blood spilled on her carpet. Or at all. "Cat, go away. Nobody called you. Although, nobody called you either, Shimun. I mean, *et tu Brutus*? You didn't even check if I'm available, what if I had some business outside, or, I don't know, a friend dropped by?"

Her cousin didn't even try to look embarrassed, his eyebrows high. "You have friends?"

Sanja almost choked on her spit. "Was that a joke at my expense?"

"You're right, I shouldn't have said that," he sighed, looking at the cat, perturbed. The mora was eyeing him with a dangerous glint in her eyes and it didn't look like she was ready to disappear. Sanja wondered if she wanted to eat him or destroy him, her form an embodiment of rage. It was an unsettling thought, so she moved to stand in front of him, facing the cat and blocking her path to Shimun.

"Go away," she said, meaning, *you can't have him.*

She didn't really expect it to work, but the cat jumped down from the windowsill, her deep eyes never leaving Sanja out of sight. *If that's what you want*, Sanja could almost imagine the words, but it was only her imagination, it had to be—wanting badly to communicate with the thing, finding something that wasn't there.

The mora disappeared again.

"Oh my God, what, it just..." Shimun was gaping at the place where the cat just vanished into thin air. Or better yet, simply stopped existing.

"Well, that was something," she tried to joke, but Shimun wasn't having it.

"What the hell, Sanja, how can you be so blasé about this? We just saw... I don't know what, a *demon,* and you're cracking jokes like it's nothing. Or no, worse than nothing, like it's your pet performing for tricks." He sounded so distraught she worried he would start yelling and alert her neighbours.

"Calm down, she did nothing. Don't be so dramatic." She sighed and sat down on the couch, wine in one hand and rubbing her eyes with the other.

"How can you still live here? Do you want that badly to be that stupid horror movie person who stays in an obviously haunted place until they inevitably die?" He paced in front of her, gesticulating wildly, like it helped with his pent up frustration. "Just, pack your bags and go... I don't know, sleep at Marija's for a few days and then we'll see. We'll figure something out."

"Look, if it's any help, I know what she is," Sanja sighed, a joke about how priests shouldn't talk about trashy movies because with the vow they ascended above the need of entertainment left unsaid in her head. He was too freaked out, and she needed to be serious with him, right now. Before he ended up calling an emergency meeting with a Pope, asking for an exorcism. "She's not a demon, but a *mora*." A pause lay pregnant with expectation between them, Sanja on the edge of the couch, waiting for his response.

Her cousin simply stood and watched her with his steely eyes.

"You don't know what that means," she came to the inevitable conclusion.

"Enlighten me, please," he said, sitting in front of her, in the same place he always sat when he came to visit. It was really a sort of habit they had, the place they sat, the wine they drank, the topics they never talked about.

"If the old tales are to be believed, she brings the nightmares while she stra... tries to suck away the energy of the sleeper. Like a, a, succubus, sort of."

"Which is a demon," he helpfully added, unimpressed.

"Okay, a bad comparison. What I wanted to say, it's not connected to the place! I know it started with me moving into this apartment, but I think, it's me she wants, and I don't know how or why, but I don't think she'd leave me alone if I went somewhere else. So, you see, it won't help! I could just end up putting someone else in danger. Imagine if I went to Marija and something happened to Dario? He's barely ten." She was surprised by how honestly concerned she sounded at that moment, dragging some resemblance of emotion from some deep pit of her brain. Mostly, she just hoped Shimun would leave her alone. To deal with this however she sees fit, without his concern and sad eyes the color of melting ice.

"And how should that make me feel better? How should the knowledge that this thing latches on your soul help me in any way?" He looked at her with a worry that felt tangible, as a living thing she could catch between her palms.

“It shouldn’t, I know. I wanted to say moving away won’t help with this thing. But I’m not giving up. I’m researching it.” It wasn’t a lie. She simply decided not to comment on dead ends and obstacles in the form of unhelpful books and Wikipedia articles.

“I’m worried for your soul, Sanja,” he said, gravely. Like proclaiming some big prophecy. Funny how he saw what the mora was doing to her as a problem, but not what Grandma had done. They both sucked energy, but only one of them was supposed to take care of her. At least he didn’t ask her to go back to Grandma, this time.

“Don’t worry. I’m already damned.” She sipped the wine. Sweet, like cherries and figs, reminding her of summer, lashes and the sea. The memory of dead Sanja floating in the deep blue water made the wine taste bad, like a nut sitting heavily in her stomach. She had to put down her glass, nauseous.

“Please, don’t talk like that,” Shimun said and crossed himself, as if the gesture held any power to stop her from blaspheming. “Besides, you know I don’t think like that.”

“Think like what?”

His face was pinched in pain. “You know fully well that I don’t believe that... gay people are condemned to Hell. Jesus is love and He said...”

“Oh for fuck’s sake, I wasn’t talking about that.” Her heart skipped for a bit. While Shimun knew about her, and was always nothing but supporting, they rarely discussed the way his Church treated people like her. Nor did she want to talk to him about how afraid she was that his support was conditional on them being cousins, and that towards everyone else he was just the same as every other priest she’d heard speaking in person. So she very purposely tried really hard not to talk with him about that part of her life. There was no point in them discussing it now. “You know what I dreamt of one night? Whom, I mean," she said quietly, looking down at her wine. The golden liquid looked like piss.

Contemplating whether or not she should relay this one particular dream to Shimun, she looked up and searched his eyes, as deep as the color of the stormy sky. Their color and shape was her own, like looking at the mirror. If she couldn't confide in him, who else could she?

"My dad. I dreamed of my dad coming to me. Older. Alive." She skipped the part where he was a vampire that attacked her. That sort of psychoanalysis wasn't what she needed from her cousin.

"Oh, Sanja..." His voice was full of unshed tears for her. She hated it. All of them, except Grandma, sounded like that when the topic of her parents came up."I'm so sorry, look, I—"

"You remember what Grandma said that last time? On Easter, I mean?" she interrupted him. He nodded, but with the uncertainty of a man who'd come unprepared to his oral exam.

The memory came unbridled to Sanja's mind. The smells of cooked ham, eggs and spring onions, blessed at the Easter mass. The oppressing presence of her relatives—uncles and aunt—and Grandma sitting in front of her at the table. The rusty golden lamp shining upon the old woman, highlighting sharp features of her cheekbones and mouth that opened up wide, showing a yellowish string of teeth, light caught at the canines. Sanja had sat there watching Grandma's mouth, how she chewed through blessed food, and downed glass upon glass of homemade walnut *rakija*. The more she'd drunk the strong alcohol and smiled her crooked yellow grin, the more Sanja had withdrawn in a tight ball of nerves, waiting for the inevitable pendulum to drop and slice through her.

The blade had come in the form of a comment thrown her way, words sharpened like a fine butcher's cleaver. Completely unprompted, as it usually goes.

"She said my father is burning in Hell for what he's done." Sanja came back to present, grounding herself on the couch. Grandma's voice was ringing in her ears, an echo of a memory hammered in her mind. "How his soul is damned. Left to the demons to torture. How I should pray for him to God, to show mercy for his poor soul. You can't tell me you don't remember that."

Shimun didn't. Maybe he hadn't even heard it. He'd been preoccupied with his kid half-siblings, sitting at the children's table most of the meal. But Sanja's uncles and aunt had heard, and they'd done nothing, said nothing. Not even when Grandma had switched to Sanja's mother—their dead sister—remembering fondly how useless she was, her biggest failure of all children. But what else could Sanja expect from her uncles and aunt—they were all just spineless puppets that swayed on their strings, Grandma's hooks latched deep in their brains. All of them trying to protect themselves, but never her.

"Well, the point I tried to make before—if he's in Hell, then him visiting me in my sleep means I'm half there anyway," Sanja said, fully aware how ridiculous that sounded. Yet, it made some twisted sense in her head. She'd felt half cursed already, even before the mora. Shimun said he was worried about her soul, but there was something pretty damning in her from the get go, twisting her insides into a putrid hole sucking out all of her will. It was sort of fitting that the mora had chosen to torture her in dreams with her dead father, whose mental illness had drawn him to slice his own wrists.

"That's not even how it works, what are you...?" Shimun was waving his hands around, like he was trying to pluck the words from the air like mulberries. "Look, I'm sorry I don't remember that, I must have... doesn't matter, look at me, look, Sanja." He crossed the empty space between them to put his hands on her cheeks, holding her face in a warm and soft embrace. For a moment she had to fight not to wince, reminding herself that he was not Grandma, that he was safe. He was trying to comfort her, not discipline her. "It's the unclean spirit that's giving you nightmares, not your dad. You're not going to Hell. Please, don't say things like that just 'cause Grandma doesn't know what she's saying most of the time."

"Doesn't know?" Sanja almost missed the last remark, but when it finally registered she moved his hands from her face and got up from the couch, to put some distance between them. She was so sick of him defending Grandma all the time. Even the little ones knew what kind of woman she was, with Dario even calling her an old hag. Behind her back, of course, but it was still better than the bootlicking Shimun—a grown ass man—was still doing to this day. "She knows exactly what she's talking about. All the time. And besides, was she lying? Tell me, what does your religion say about suicide? Who taught her those things about Hell?"

"That's not... the point... she, I mean," he was grasping for words, and gaping like a fish on dry land. "She shouldn't tell it like that. But! She's just... old and angry because she loved your parents and she lost them both so soon, and *he left you*... she knows she can't do anything for him... there is no amount of praying..."

"She's... she loved them? *Oh my God,* Shimun, you're delusional!" Sanja didn't know whether to cry or to laugh. Grandma forgot half the time Sanja's dad existed, and when she talked about him it was mostly in derision. Or she used him to pass some sort of judgement at Sanja's mother, her own daughter that—in Grandma's mind—failed to keep her husband happy or otherwise he wouldn't have killed himself. If there had truly been a time she cared for her son-in-law, it was so corroded with years it had turned into something opposite of love. Whatever feelings she'd had for Sanja's mother, on other hand... the three of them had lived together before her mother's death, and Sanja was old enough to understand that what they had wasn't love, or concern. It was ugly, twisted and bitter. A hungry sort of resentment in which Grandma tried so very hard to destroy Sanja's mom. For whatever reason, though, Sanja still didn't really understand. Nor did she need to. "You don't know, is it possible that you don't? Do you really believe all this nonsense you said? I mean, I know you didn't live with her all the time. Still, I thought you had a better grasp of her personality than this. You saw what she did to me! For God's sake, you're the one she goes to for confessions, and you knew, you knew how she raised me!"

"She was strict, I know, please calm down, it was just to protect you in the only way she knew how!"

"To protect me?" She was laughing now, out loud, with an ugly smile on her lips and her eyes closed so she wouldn't cry. She closed her fists, too, so she wouldn't take the wine glass from the table and throw it with force at the wall.

"She was worried about you, tried to protect you, and it was how her parents and grandparents had raised her, just because we know better now..."

"You know what? I'm tired, you should go." And she wasn't even lying. The little they'd spoken to each other had squeezed all the energy from her and dumped it in the trash. Her body was laden with heavy chains of rage, frustration and resignation. The only thing she needed right now was comfort, not even the reassurance that her father wasn't being tortured for the whole eternity, just for someone to listen to her pain. To understand why she's so messed up, even without the mora's work.

Shimun's expression looked like she'd slapped him on both cheeks, but she couldn't care. "Please, I'm sorry if I'd upset you, I thought we could talk about the actual *evil thing* and–"

"We did. Just now. But you should go," she repeated.

He finally walked to the doors, looking dejected with his slumped shoulders and heavy steps. If he hoped his pathetic look would make her relent, he was sorely mistaken. She was too drained to fight, to think, to even try to make him understand her position. Both of his parents, after all, were still alive. And he was Grandma's favorite. Why would she think he could ever relate to her?

After their little talk, she just wanted to get drunk and sleep, even if that meant she'd dream. Maybe her dad was waiting for her there. What were the chances that the mora would conjure him again? Sanja didn't even care if he drank all of her blood, before disappearing again in the morning.

Sanja abruptly stopped at the doors, remembering something Shimun had said earlier. "He didn't *leave* me, like getting up and driving away, and don't you dare say something like that again." She was getting angry again, and decided to let it all out. "My dad was depressed. He was sick and he needed real help, doctor sort of help. So don't you dare. If you're not going to bash our grandpa for dying of cancer, you're not going to talk ill of my dad. Understand?" For a moment she thought Shimun would be foolish enough to try and dissuade her, but he closed his mouth and nodded. Smart enough, it seemed.

"I'm sorry," he told her in the end.

"I know."

She still closed the doors to his face instead of telling him all sorts of things, like, *I know you care*, and *I'll take care of this thing*. He didn't deserve to listen to any of her reassurances.

Out of the blue, Sanja wondered if her monster drank alcohol.

* * *

She didn't. Of course she didn't. But the mora watched her through the night, while Sanja slowly sipped on her wine as she sat on the couch and ate cheese. She felt really classy like that, the yellowish strips of Gouda haphazardly cut with too small a knife. Through the window she could hear whistles and drums, but had no clue what the hell was happening in the streets nor had any wish to find out.

Ta dam ta dam ta dam banged in her ears, a rhythm of life.

"What kind of dreams are you preparing for me tonight? Am I dreaming right now?" She asked the woman standing by her side, so close that Sanja could lean over the couch and touch her ghastly leg. Silence was the only answer she got. "Will I find out that I'm in Hell and those are demons playing the drums, in a welcoming procession for my soul? Do they have that there? Do you even know?"

The woman just watched, her long black hair cascading on her back and obfuscating half of her face from the front. *Ta dam ta dam ta dam.* Was that the beating of Sanja's heart or noises outside?

"Why won't you talk to me? Am I not interesting enough? I could learn sign language if I have to." She knew she was being silly, and really imprudent. But when was she ever cautious with this thing in her apartment? Why start now? Grandma would say she was looking for trouble, and whatever happened was her own damn fault.

Maybe she should just lie down and close her eyes, letting the *ta dam ta dam ta dam* to put her to sleep like a lullaby.

"We must've been entertaining to watch. I wish I was only a spectator of my life and not the main actor. It sucks. Like you. *Why are you always silent*?" Sanja lamented, letting her discomfort out in the open. "Is there a horror award in the afterlife, or supernatural planes, or whatever the hell you crawled out?"

The mora's silence was like a light touch of moonlight on her skin. She could catch it and tattoo it on the insides of her eyelids, like fireworks of golden sparks. The shouts and drums and whistles were still audible outside, but only a background noise, too far away.

"Fine, be the creepy silent lurker if you must. I hope you have fun." Looking was hard. The room was tilting to the right, her stomach upset, a feeling similar to standing on a slippery slope. She'd read a book with the same title once upon a time. Hidden under the quilt, using a small flashlight, because it was one of the forbidden novels. Grandma had confiscated her library card but, thankfully, the librarians knew her and were always giving her new books even when they weren't on her approved list. And it was a good thing, because Sanja understood all too well what she was reading about, and she knew, just like the kids in the books, what missing parents felt like and that the world was a quiet and dangerous place. That there was no help coming to them, but it was still hard not to hope for happier days.

Her breathing was becoming shallow, and there was something growing in her lungs. A tree, huge, green and red; she could see it in her mind. Its branches were twisting inside her chest, wanting to burst out and grow, reaching for the stars dripping with blood. The drums intensified. *Ta dam ta dam ta dam.*

Completely taut, her body was slowly breaking—cracking open up like a ripe fig in two pieces with maggots squirming inside. With a dark curtain over her eyes, sightless, she could intensely feel the old cuts and hits, the points where the walnut whip had made contact, the old bruises. A whole canvas of painted tears. The freezing pain on her skin where cold water had hit her, once upon a time. Because she'd made a mess of her Sunday clothes and needed to be cleaned. Because there were spots all over her, which screamed *disgrace*. The shame was nothing compared to pounding of *ta dam ta dam TA DAM*! The drums, telling her something, but the meaning still slipping between her fingers like sand.

Arms, cold arms. Squeezing in hard like some twisted CPR. She should open her eyes, *when did she close them*? She should do something. Anything but lying on her back, *why was she lying down?* With a lithe body covering hers, the touch so intimate. There was a leg between her own two, naked skin clammy upon contact, creating friction with movement. *It wasn't right. Not like this*, whispered something in her ear, a memory of what this sort of embrace should feel like. Sanja was fighting through the tar weighing down her eyes, panic slowly overtaking her in waves. Gradually, she managed to open her eyes, with sheer strength of will. To the sight of a woman straddling her and pushing down on her chest like she wanted to break her ribs and tear out her heart with nothing but her bare hands.

Sanja tried to raise her own arms and push the woman away, get up, or jerk her legs, but nothing worked. She was paralysed from the neck down. And when the mora moved, slowly sliding down towards Sanja's face, close enough to kiss her, and still with no air coming from her mouth, Sanja decided to let go of everything—of the age old fear fermenting in her brain like stale wine, of the panic overcoming her senses and muddying reality.

Of the idea that she could ever breathe with full lungs.

Feeling lightless, like a feather blown on the wind, Sanja withdrew into the dark place, hidden deeply inside her brain, where she stored memories that burned. The old saying that life flashed before your eyes came to her mind, for a moment, before Sanja drowned in her own history.

Remembering the body shattered like a porcelain doll, neck and bones broken, blood flowing from the smashed skull, watering the ground and turning the green grass the color of muted puke. With that vision, she could feel it again, all of it, slowly getting out of its closed box—the way she'd cried in despair when her Grandma stripped her of clothes and bathed her with a water hose, in the yard where neighbours and passers by could see her naked trembling. The burning pain of a sudden slap to the face when her oldest uncle had surprised her one day, never before hitting her like that. She remembered the slap, but not what she'd said to warrant it at the diner table.

The feeling of being lost in the crowd, surrounded by relatives and strangers alike, but unable to see her dad anywhere, crying in her little white dress, an equally white chrysanthemum in her hand. She'd forgotten about that.

Forgotten how she'd stood at the bathroom doors and watched blood turning into a river from the sliced skin of the arms that used to carry her around. She'd almost slipped when she stumbled upon it, but instead got stuck in place, that lake of blood glued to her slipper, mesmerised by the way her father was leaning over the tub, the whiteness of the enamel marred with the red tears dripping from his flesh. A fly danced on her father's glassy eyes. She'd forgotten that, but not anymore. Nor the way her mother cried while cleaning Sanja's little blood soaked slipper before screaming into the night.

And then, much later, she was standing again, in a different white dress with a different white flower in hands, and there were her uncles and aunt—with her cousins Shimun and Marija at their legs—making sad faces at the grave, all remorseful over Sanja's dead mother's coffin, but completely useless while she was still alive. And Sanja wanted to rage and scream and light thousand candles to burn it all to ground even though she couldn't define what she meant by *all*. The graveyard? Her family? The corpses of her parents? The world, perhaps? Shimun tried to cheer her up, but he failed, and she started to wail so hard that Grandma locked her in a cold, lightless room, to weep alone. And in the darkness, she could hear loud voices of men—her uncles—their angry shouting, trashing and slaps. Except she wasn't really alone at that point, oh now. Now she knew better.

It was already there—that fear that didn't give her a moment of peace, enveloping her in a tight embrace, never again letting her get away. She awakened with it, brushed her teeth with it at her shoulders, walked outside hand in hand with it. It was there every time Grandma came at her with the walnut branch. It was there when she had to carefully choose words at her job so she wouldn't accidentally come out to a wrong teacher or a parent who'd make it harder for her to work, or impossible at all. Every time she had to lie about why she didn't have a partner, when all her peers had boyfriends or husbands, when she knew they all believed something was seriously wrong with her, as if being alone was the same as being a leper. The fear that she would end up forever alone, a living corpse waddling through life with a broken oar. That she would continue to live with her Grandma's shadow, even after getting away. That shadow was a constant in her life and it took so much of the space that there was no room for anybody else.

So she walked alone, and sat alone, and worked alone, talking with her colleagues but never truly speaking. Because if she said what she truly felt, what she truly thought, if they learned who she truly was, there would be reckoning.

Stick and stones and broken bones, and slaps and lost jobs, and shame, the constant shame of standing naked in the freezing water, begging it to stop, saying she didn't mean to get dirty, never meaning to do anything at all. And yet it never stopped.

It became so heavy on her mind, that she let it all out—the memories, the pain, the constant fear in her brain—in a voiceless scream. Everything she had under lock and key, the ugly, deformed lump in her chest, breaking her breaths.

Abruptly, she felt a sensation of falling upwards and her vision uncontrollably switched sides.

She wasn't in her body anymore.

She wasn't breathing—it was the first thing that came to her mind. The second was the fact that she was looking through a milky white haze, watching down on her own paralysed body. Which was still gasping for air, silently choking under those strange arms she now had. She tried to move away, to stop her new body from crushing her old one to death, not really wanting to die. Not wanting to become a rotting corpse on the couch for her cousins to find, with empty bottles of wine and discarded cheese on the floor. She was tired of a life of pain and fear, of existing, even, but it wasn't fair. It shouldn't end like this for her. With her arms squeezing her own life, as if suicide were something passed down through genes.

An image flashed through her mind—Shimun sadly standing over her dead body, murmuring a prayer, but with the face of someone who knew he'd been right all along. Her grandmother would let a tear or two at the funeral, talking how it was all that bad blood, and that she'd tried so hard to give her grandchild a good life but, ultimately, there wasn't a thing she could've done to prevent poor Sanja's untimely death. And how now it was too late for her soul, forever lost in the depths of Hell.

At that thought, with Grandma's face in her mind, anger erupted from Sanja, unbridled. A feeling of free fall and then—a connection, a sense of her own body and skin. Fighting for air, she let out a scream, her paralysed body suddenly awaking with the strength of a boulder rolling down the hill. Breaking through paralysis, she punched and turned and gripped and growled like some feral thing let out of the cage. There wasn't any sense, her mind completely blank, her sight soaked in red.

Something moved and cut through her gaze. She wasn't certain what it was, but in the end, the result was the same. She stopped. Her teeth hurt from being gritten too hard. Her breaths were loud and quick, with sweat dripping from her forehead like she'd run for a thousand miles. And underneath her, pinned to the floor, was a motionless body of the mora, frozen in... shock? Fear?

Sanja could see her own palms over the other woman's neck, squeezing hard, like it was a lemon in her fist. The mora wasn't breathing in the first place, so Sanja couldn't choke her to death, but she tried, oh how she squeezed and hurt back. The woman under her arms was grasping and trashing, her eyes bugging like they would pop out of the head, watching her in a manner Sanja knew to her core.

It wasn't the sort of look she wanted to see directed at her, and *yet*...

For a moment, she was tempted to experiment.

But the memory of seeing her own body getting smothered to death, while she'd been looking through the mora's eyes, closed down the angry turmoil inside her.

With a scorching pain in her arms, she opened her palms and slowly disentangled herself from the mora. She didn't know how they'd ended up on the floor, or in what moment she'd managed to overpower her formidable roommate. Watching the mora moving quickly away from her and hugging her own legs, in a silent search for comfort that Sanja could understand, she felt terrible.

Which was really stupid, given that the mora had *started* it. But still.

The unnaturally pale body was crisscrossed with scratches and bite marks, marring the otherwise unblemished skin. Sanja swallowed guilt with a side of rotten blood she'd gotten on her tongue. Thin lines that drew dark blood left a trail on the other woman's face, showing where Sanja had tried—at some point, she didn't even remember it, it all happened in such a rush—to claw out her eyes. And when she looked on her own fists, she could see strange scraps of skin under her nails.

"Well, this got awkward." Sanja was watching the woman, eye to eye. Still so close. Confusion crawled across the mora's face, just like the centipede that was currently tip-toeing on the far wall, probably trying to stay outside of whatever was happening between two women on the floor. It seemed that the mora wasn't certain what had just transpired and didn't know what to expect next. Like Sanja was the monster between the two of them. More time passed, marked only by loud bangs of the clock on the wall. She remembered hearing drums, but everything was silent again sadly. Maybe she'd truly dreamt that.

With the finality of a kid failing a class, she managed to calm herself and wipe down the sweaty palms on her legs.

"You think you're the first monster in my life?" Sanja's voice sounded strange in her ears, like hearing yourself on the radio, airing from the fifth circle of Hell. But she sat with her head held high, looking straight at the woman's eyes, unafraid. Refusing to feel guilt over what she'd done. "You're not even the worst of them."

The mora blinked and looked away. Was the creature unable to handle the sight of her? Was Sanja so damned not even malevolent entities could stand her?

"I'm not dying and you're not feeding on me. Which means we're at a sort of an impasse." Sanja moved toward the woman and she cowered. The satisfaction over that revelation was dark but sweet. She'll not let the mora break her. Never again. "I don't know what you're trying to do, whether you're trying to scare me away, or if you *just* enjoy torturing me. But enough is enough." The woman didn't answer, but Sanja knew the look in her eyes. Light shone back from dark irises in fear, and Sanja could see the shape of her own body reflected there. "If we have to live together, there will be rules. You're not doing this again—or, I swear to God above and the Devil in the pits of Hell, I will find a way to kill you and mount your dead lungs as a trophy above my bed."

There was no fear left in her, drained in the fight. Sanja was ready for whatever the woman might do next. Even if it was just talking, if there even was a way for them to communicate. So she waited, and waited, and the woman blinked out of the space like she'd never even been there.

5

It would be so, so easy to make herself believe that she imagined everything, and that there wasn't actually a mora that haunted her dreams, that it was just her brain, eaten away with past trauma, acting out. The dark purple bruise on her chest disagreed with that idea.

She trailed the edges of the deep color on her skin, feeling the ribcage where it closed over her heart, protecting it. She breathed in, breathed out. Again, and again, before the alarm sounding in her kitchen made her hastily throw a shirt over herself, brown like mud and her hair, covering up the purple under it.

* * *

Instagram was full of pictures of Rex—a shaggy black dog with goofy face, one of those 'Domestic Mutts' with no papers or family trees, but that once maybe had a drop of a regal german shepherd's blood.

Ana was scrolling down her grid and showing her pictures, while Sanja tried really hard to smile and give the occasional appropriate response, to act like a human being and not a creepy, haunted, porcelain baby doll that kills owners in their sleep. She almost *forgot*. After getting so excited over this coffee date—of sorts, but not really a date, of course—the incident with the mora almost made her miss it completely. Thankfully, Ana had seen her at the school before she could disappear hastily after her lectures. For that one moment—while Ana was waiting for Sanja to take her things—everything was brighter and lighter, and she thought she could put last night behind her. But now, it was hard to concentrate.

Coffee had no taste, her clothes felt too heavy on her, the place smelled of burned cigarettes, and the world was dipped in a bucket full of gray paint. Even other people, smiling and talking through their *cappuccinos* and *macchiatos*, looked dimmed to her eyes and distant, shrouded in distorted sounds. Even Ana, who usually looked like sunset was caught in her ruddy hair, was somewhat dulled with her colors, like everything had bled away; faded red leaving only rust.

But Sanja *will* get through this, she decided, forcing her face muscles to form a smile, even if she had to tear the words out of her mouth with tongs, like teeth.

"So, can I see yours? Cat, I mean! Poe, was it?" The sudden question broke through Sanja's sluggish thoughts. The coffee shop was bursting with life on its busy street, with everyone being on a coffee break at any given time in the day. And still, Sanja felt as if nothing was real and the server would come with a receipt to inform her she was still sleeping and it's time to wake up for work. Only to come to the school and learn that Ana had already moved on from the job, to another school.

Someone's phone rang, the tone the same as her alarm and Sanja blanched. But she didn't wake up. She wasn't sleeping, everything was alright. Her coffee was muddy brown, with burned aftertaste, and she clung to it as an anchor for her sanity.

"Uh? Oh." Ana was watching her with anticipation, and Sanja felt like her students must feel when she asked them a question. And she was expecting pictures of Sanja's very regular *cat*, because that's what normal people did. They took pictures of their pets. And then showed them to other people.

But Sanja wasn't a normal person, nor did she own a cat of any sorts. She only had a mora, sometimes masquerading as a cat, but that wasn't something she could say on their first *coffee* date. Could she even take a photo of it or would it be invisible for the camera, like a vampire in the mirrors? Of course, vampires weren't real, and you couldn't get ghosts to show on photos, so she wasn't sure what would happen if she tried to capture the mora with modern technology. "No... er... my phone had a full memory card so I had to back up all the photos on my laptop. You know. And I don't really do social media. So..." she trailed away, hoping Ana wouldn't be able to see the notification for full memory on her phone, persistently trying to make her fix it for months now.

"Oh. Some other time, maybe?" Ana made an effort not to sound disappointed, and Sanja couldn't help but feel like a failure. She couldn't even lie properly, making nice girls sad instead, with the lack of cute cat pictures.

"Sure... anyway, how's job hunting going?" *Really smooth, Sanja. Nothing like changing the subject.* At least she picked something relatively normal, and not weird. But also quite boring and unimaginative. What will come out of her mouth next? Something about the weather?

"Unfortunately, not really well..." And now Ana sounded all out dispirited, after being so happy and uplifting before, and Sanja wanted to bang her head against the desk. "Only one school in town is looking for a math teacher, but only as a substitute. Of course, it could still turn out to be maternity leave, which would be great."

"Ah, yeah. It always starts like that. And before you know it, you're secure for at least two years."

She could have continued in this matter, saying something about her own experience in the school system—how coming as a substitute for a teacher that broke her leg had turned into the happy coincidence of a permanent position when another teacher, from the same school, retired a few weeks later—but felt like a sure way to bore Ana to death.

The conversation stilted and Sanja played with her cup of *macchiato* trying to find a way to steer the topic away from the job or schools or children. And to keep them talking. *Why is this so hard?* She used to do this, have friends, hang out with them. Even date. Her first few years at college were a social renaissance. But time passed; a few bad break ups, an emotionally taxing transition from college to substituting to apartment hunting—it turned her into a neglectful friend who had a hard time showing up somewhere or picking up the phone. Before she knew it, the only people visiting her were her cousins. Her friends had moved on. *Why wouldn't they?* a voice whispered in her head. Her brain hurt, and sluggish thoughts didn't help, making a fight out of a simple chat.

"I'm sorry, I know this question is sort of lame, but... are you okay? You look like—"

"Like roadkill?" Sanja tried to joke, hiding the hurt. Ana smiled, but it would appear her eyes didn't get the memo. Sanja's stomach clenched. "I'm just tired, that's all." She considered lying and telling everything was okay, but discarded it, fully aware not even an Oscar winning actor would be able to pull it off if he looked like she did at the moment. "Couldn't sleep all night so I pretty much feel like I'm sleepwalking. I'm sorry, I'm not the best company right now." *Or ever, really,* the same voice cheerfully added. It sounded suspiciously like Grandma, so she ignored it as best as she could, drinking bitter coffee to wash it away.

"No, no, please don't apologize. Why didn't you say anything? You should've gone straight home, tried to get some sleep! Not let me drag you out for coffee. Oh my... *coffee*!" Ana spat the last word out like a curse. "Why are you drinking this if you're having troubles sleeping?!" Ana sounded so indignant Sanja couldn't help herself. She smiled. An actual, real smile managed to crawl on her face.

"Nah, it's fine, really." Upon seeing Ana's incredulous look she amended, "Okay, not fine, but honestly, I'm actually glad that you dragged me out. It's..." she contemplated truths and lies, trying to find what combination fit the most, "a nice thing. You know, sitting here, talking. Even though I'm tired. But it feels like everything in my life recently revolves around either work or... some problems I have at home, so... this is nice, is what I want to say."

She knew she should've kept her mouth shut as soon as worry crept into Ana's kind eyes. Now, her explanation will open a flood of other questions, ones she didn't have an answer to. Or, at least, she had no answers that wouldn't paint her like a madwoman in front of Ana.

"You know, if you want to talk, I'm here, listening. And this isn't just a platitude. I really mean it. I know we don't know each other really well, but still. My ears are all yours." And there were lovely ears, but Sanja wasn't sure if she should take that offer. Where would she even start? *You see, it all began one day when my grandpa's ghost visited me in the yard...* Which really wasn't the truth, it had begun even before that, with her parents meeting, which ultimately ended in the unfortunate consequence of her conception and birth.

She should say 'thank you', switch the subject or pay for coffee and run away. Instead, the words started slowly leaking from her mouth like miasma. "I have a problem with nightmares. That's why I can't sleep. It sounds so childish, not like something a grown woman should have a problem with."

An exasperated laugh managed to get away from her, ringing hollow in the air between them. She didn't want to look completely pathetic in front of the other girl, but still. She braced herself and continued.

"But these particular dreams, they sort of managed to drag out some repressed memories. And those not that repressed, but still unwelcome. I didn't have the happiest childhood, you see. I... I'm not sure if I should be telling you this, I mean, we barely know each other, but, if you really want to know..." She took a deep breath, preparing herself for a story she didn't tell strangers for years. "See, my dad comited suicide when I was four, and apparently it was me who found him. His bo... well, you know." Once it started, the word vomit flew, without a dam to stop it. And with the way Ana listened to her carefully, fully immersed in Sanja's story, her eyes opening wide in surprise, maybe she didn't even want to stop talking. "And then later, when I was ten, my mother had an accident. She died. At that point we were living with Grandma, because ever since dad's death, mom really had a hard time, and it was supposed to help. It didn't. Grandma is... well, strict. Her standards are impossible to please. I really think she managed to make life worse for mom, not better, but you know how it goes. We didn't have a lot of money, with mom working as a cashier and with dad dead. Anyway, my point is, Grandma's not the cuddly, warm old woman from stories; the sort that should spring in your mind when you hear the word *grandma*. The *archetypal* one, who bakes cookies and tells you stories. Well, she did bake cookies and tell stories, but hers were cautionary tales of children that didn't behave, of sins and Hell, of what happens to *loose* women. Her definition of a loose woman was really everything you could possibly do, wrong or not. It was enough to be a woman and..." Sanja made a gesture with her arm, like trying to chase away invisible flies.

"Breathe?" Ana helpfully filled in. "Yeah, I know the type." Her eyes and mouth suddenly had a sharpness to them, one Sanja didn't see before. Ever since they've met, she's always thought of Ana as someone made of light brushstrokes, a painting of a mellow fairy hidden in the woods, dancing in the warm sun rays. Right now, she was all angles, the sharpened blade made for skinning animals, just a hint of harsh winter nights caught in a woodcut. Was she angry? On Sanja's behalf? Drymouthed, Sanja turned her gaze to her coffee, trying to get away from that intense look. Knowing she didn't deserve it—why would she? "You stayed with your grandma?"

"Yeah. With her and her rules and her... doesn't matter what, anyway. I'm like those orphans from children's literature who have to go through hardships and cruel situations. But instead of defeating the evil grownups and learning some deep truths about humans and life while growing up, I just... grew up. There were no monsters slayed in my story. No evil witch burned in the oven. Even the Boudelaires get to watch Count Olaf die in the end. But I don't. I can't run away from my family." She shrugged, unwilling to say any more on the subject. She somehow, simultaneously, felt worse than before and better, too, like some huge rock had rolled off her shoulders, only to crush her feet. Her past weighed her down. This amount of emotional baggage couldn't make her look good in Ana's eyes. There was no way this sunshine woman would want to hang around a person this messed up.

A hand suddenly showed up on hers, now gripping a cup of cold coffee. The striking contrast between the two hands caught her unaware. Was she really that pale, almost white, like a clean bed sheet from the TV commercials? Like she hadn't seen the sun for decades; worse than any Scandinavian tourist on Croatian beaches in summer.

Sanja found the other girl's eyes full with emotion she couldn't really name. She felt like she should know, but the meaning slipped away like smoke from a cigarette. Uncomfortable in the intensity of that look, she dragged away her gaze, hoping Ana won't see the desperation in her face.

"I'm so sorry for your loss," Ana's voice was quiet but firm. "There's nothing to be ashamed of. All of us have a few skeletons in our closets," she said through a small smile, but in a completely serious tone. Sanja's heart started beating faster. "Thank you for telling me this. I know it couldn't have been easy. And listen, about your nightmares, it's not a failure on your part if you have them, or if you're unable to deal with them. You've lived through some heavy stuff, losing your parents so young and in such a way..."

Sanja felt like complete shit. By obfuscating the truth, sharing only a part of it, she'd managed to stir Ana in the wrong direction with her conclusions. There was nothing natural about her nightmares. They weren't a symptom of a tortured mind. There was a very real monster causing them; dredging all of the grime from her past out in the present.

"Are you seeing someone, if you don't mind me asking? Not seeing as in *dating*," Ana quickly amended, "although you can answer that if you want," a nervous smile accompanied it, before she managed to get serious again. "I meant like a therapist sort of way."

"No," Sanja mumbled, wondering briefly about the slip, but trying not to read too much into it. No amount of talking will help with a mora living in her apartment or her Grandma living in her mind.

Ana nodded like she wasn't really surprised. "Maybe it would help. Look, I know there's a... stigma about the whole therapy thing, but think about it. It really helps to talk to a professional." For a moment, Ana looked like she was warring with herself, contemplating whether she should say something or not. In the end, she very obviously braced herself, straightening in her seat and continued talking. "You know, my ex-girlfriend had a problem with anxiety," the words were quick like a stream in a spring, and Sanja almost didn't catch them. When she did, she very, very carefully fixed her face in a blank look, not letting the sudden turmoil of eagerness and dread to be even glimpsed at outside. "She had panic attacks, sometimes quite bad. She was seeing this really god doctor who helped her deal with it. The doctor isn't judgy at all. She's a woman too, in her late forties, has that sort of kind and understanding face. My ex wouldn't be able to go to anyone who looked threatening in any way. And really, if you had a problem with eyesight you would go to an eye specialist, wouldn't you? It's the same. I know you didn't ask me for advice, but think about it. Okay?"

Sanja was still stuck on the part of the *ex-girlfriend*, but not stuck enough to miss the similarity with what Ana was saying to her, and what Sanja herself had told Shimun about her father needing help. But she wasn't that depressed, wasn't even suicidal, and her demons were real. She wondered for a moment if her dad had felt the same way until, one day, he just sliced his wrists.

How do you get to that point? Did he know what he would do upon getting up that morning; while he was fixing her breakfast before going to work? Did he think about how it was the last breakfast they'll have together? Or did it happen spontaneously? A moment that felt just like any other moment in his life, when something snapped?

Ana was waiting for an answer, and since Sanja had remarkably managed to paint herself as someone who should really seek help for her mental health, she didn't want to end up looking as an ignorant asshole on top of that. So she nodded and took down the name and phone number of the therapist, not really sure what she'll do with it, except save it on her phone. It's not like it would help with her mora situation, but maybe it would help with Ana's opinion about the lost lonely orphan she'd once gone on a coffee date with.

* * *

Jesus knows all. Sanja dumbfoundedly watched the sentence that one of her students had written on white paper, her pen poised for an attack. Really, of all the things she'd seen written in exams, this was definitely the ultimate winner for the best *worst* answer ever. She shortly debated whether she should take a pic of it and send it to Ana for a laugh, but then stopped dead in the conclusion that it was pointless. After their conversation the other day had taken a drastic turn into a sob story of her life, could she really just send her a joke, as if nothing had happened? Like she didn't open her gut and showed the other girl how dark her insides were?

Jesus maybe knows all, but you don't, she wrote instead in her red pen, next to a huge slash she'd made over the answer, almost making a tear in the paper under her fingers.

The cat meowed behind her, the one she didn't have. Her stomach clenched in response.

"Well, well, well... look who decided to show up." She turned back in her seat, deliberately slow, and saw the cat watching her with wary attention. Sanja gripped the edge of her chair, not really ready to deal with mora's nonsense, conjuring an air of confidence to put on her face like a mask. It wasn't that hard to fake it; she did it everyday in class. And the last time they'd clashed, Sanja was the one who came out on top in their fight, so maybe the mora would be more careful this time. In fact, who knows, maybe the mora would now finally leave her alone. No such luck, of course.

She could still taste blood on her tongue. She could still feel pain when she touched the purple spots on her chest.

She could still see the mora sitting—frightened and dazed, beaten and bloodied—on the floor.

Sanja turned back to her stack of exams, swallowing sour regret and a touch of anger at herself for feeling like that in the first place. At least forty five papers out of sixty three were waiting on the table for her to grade, and she didn't have time for any kind of distraction. And it was mora who'd started it. How many times does she need to remind herself of that fact? So why did she feel like absolute trash? She was simply protecting herself.

"What do you want?" Sanja asked eventually. She wasn't really expecting a reply, but there was nothing else for her to do, as tired as she was of feeling strongly again—even if it was only the misplaced regret—after being completely empty inside for the whole day. The cat meowed again, like she was trying to answer her after all, but was unable to actually communicate.

Sanja sighed and rubbed her eyes. There was sawdust under them, and the thought of going back to grading exams filled her with bile. She should take a break. It was as good a moment as any. Seeing the cat again reminded her of the particular question Ana had asked and, on a whim, she took out her phone and snapped a quick picture. *How curious,* she thought, watching the photo. It would appear that you *could* actually photograph a supernatural creature—only, it looked like a regular black cat with a little bit of a white fur below the neck. *Behold, the evil that brings me nightmares every night and tries to choke me.* She could show the whole world this proof that folk tales were real, and they would reply: *It's a cat Sanja, a cute, albeit boring domestic cat. Maybe you should go and see a shrink.*

She played with the phone in her hand for a moment and then made the drastic decision and shared the photo with Ana. It was a stupid photo. The cat didn't even look especially cute in it, simply sitting on the floor, looking at the lens like she thought Sanja had lost her mind. She probably did, since she'd sent it. And without saying a word to the other woman after their coffee date, too. Trying to lessen the weirdo flavor, she added: *I believe I owed you a photo.* Great, now she sounded too anal. *Poe says hi btw :)* She sent in addition, and her throat knotted in a lump.

The mora was still there, looking at her with that burning eyes, but otherwise not doing anything at all. Sitting on the dusty floor...

The floor. The unclean, unmopped floor. Was it visible in the photo that Sanja hadn't really swept the house for the days? Or was it weeks now?

She dropped the phone on the table and stood up. "Do you want to see something?"

She didn't wait for an answer. What she really wanted was to delete the messages she'd sent, but then Ana would see that she'd deleted something, and ask what it was. Sanja decided to simply stop thinking about what she did, about the phone, about the state of her floor. She wasn't running. She simply went to the other room. It was just that, in her small studio, she wouldn't be able to hear the notifications, neither the loudness of the ping nor the deafening silence of the lack of an answer.

Surprisingly, or maybe not so much, the cat followed her.

Once she reached the studio, Sanja took a deep breath. There was nothing in that room except her old works.

"Have you been here before? I don't know when was the last time I... Oh, wait, I ironed my shirt here the other day. Nevermind. I tried to be all moody with my grave 'the last time' speech and failed." The cat appeared to be unimpressed. Sanja sighed and went to her paintings. Each new step weighed more than the last. The pieces were stored facing the wall, and yet it felt like they were watching her. Judging her.

She started going through a stack, slowly turning them towards the room, one by one.

"Here, you can see one of my early ones." The abandoned bath was overflowing with bloodied water spilling from its edge, splattering on the floor. There were bloody footprints too, going into the tub. "I'd forgotten that I was there, you know. Thought that I was being all symbolic and deep, painting the tub without the body, only blood to imply what had happened there. But I was there. I found him. I saw him. Maybe I chose to paint it without him because I'd also forgotten what he looked like. Mom burned all his pictures, too angry at him for leaving her, I guess. I only remember him in a vague sense. A beard. A smile. As a warm brown color." These few sensations were the only thing left to her from her dad. Looking at the painting now, Sanja realized she had never tried to paint any of the happy or loving memories, but instead painted this moment of utmost dread. Sadness was too tremendous to even try to comprehend it at that moment, so she tried to shake the feeling away; minimise the hurt she felt.

"Anyway, the bloody footprints were supposed to symbolise him going to his death. But it was probably just my subconscious playing tricks, because you see, after our... dance the other night, I remembered that day. I'd accidentally stepped in his blood. I was the one that left the bloody trails... Anyway, this isn't really even that good work. Like I said, early one."

The cat sat at her feet and watched the painting with a power of concentration that Sanja's students could be jealous of. Sanja smiled to herself and continued her private little show and tell.

The next canvas showed an old woman eating the heart from the shattered ribcage of a young one, who lay mangled on the ground. White bones protruded from ruptures in the skin. "Portraits of my Grandma and mom. Self explanatory, I think."

It was raining that day. She didn't paint the rain. Didn't try to catch what her mother had really looked like on the pavement. Wasn't interested in the realism of the broken neck and smashed skull. Instead, it was Grandma who was in the focus of the painting; her hungry, predatory look and sharp teeth biting into the bloody heart.

"They were fighting, like always. Grandma wasn't happy with the way mom cleaned the windows. She found them unsatisfactory. But really, it was all a farce. Just a pretext so she could scream at how useless she was."

Sanja wasn't certain why she was telling this to the mora. But there was a deep need inside her, to show someone her work, to remember it properly. Not just as a canvases stacked against the wall in the corner of the room. A living story, the one she'd tried to bury years ago. The one she'd *managed* to leave behind, until a pesky mora came along and dragged it up.

"I don't know why she thought it was a good idea to try to clean them on a rainy day. *Who* cleans *windows* while it's *raining* outside? I mean, you can't, it's pointless. It's insane. I don't know if she was simply fed up with

Grandma and wanted to make a statement, make her shut up, or whatever. I just know she must've been distraught."

It was an accident, Grandma had said. Sanja knew better. It didn't matter if her mother lost balance standing on a shaky stool—trying to get to the top of the window where, apparently, the offending dirty spots were—Sanja always blamed Grandma for it. She'd pushed mom, maybe not physically, out of the window, but as good as. Guilty as charged, and yet everybody acted like it was an unfortunate tragedy.

"We lived on the seventh floor. Do you know what it sounds like when a body hits the ground after free fall for seven stories? Because I do."

She was in the next room when it happened, but still she'd heard it, as loud and clear as the fighting beforehand. Running to the window, she'd thought she would see a busted chair, something sacrificed in the fight between the two women. Instead, it was the blurry shape of her mother's broken body lying on the ground.

Sanja had ran outside before Grandma could stop her. Later, they had to physically drag her away from her mother's side. She didn't scream. She didn't blink. She just sat there, drinking in the bulging bones like flowers growing from mom's body and the chunks of brain matter scattered on the ground.

Shaking her head, Sanja dispelled the memory and reached for the next painting.

The third one was a picture in charcoal of a man with a rooster's head, human testicles hanging from his beak. "One of my uncles; the oldest one. An allegory of sorts. You can clearly see how immature I was, working with such basic symbolism. Lazy. This one was better," she showed the cat the fourth, a picture of a young man—Shimun—crucified on top of an older man's body; his dad. Grandma had hoped her second son would become a priest, bringing honor and prestige to the family. But uncle Ante—Shimun's dad—loved women too much, even married twice, rather than taking the vow. So it was up to Shimun to redeem his father and succeed where the other man had failed in his mother's eyes. When they were young, Sanja had asked him if he was absolutely sure it was something he wanted to do and not just the actions of a boy trying to make his Grandma proud. Shimun was adamant that it was his calling. But she still believed that it was their Grandma's voice he heard, not God's.

And so the show went on, turning away from her family to the world in general—dead piglets sleeping in piles of rotten mellons; a mountain screaming in agony; withered white mums growing from a mutated, two headed rat; buildings crying centipedes with human teeth instead of legs.

And in the end, there was a huge canvas with human bodies stitched together into one colossal ball, their faces frozen in agony and screams. In the middle of that sewn-up pile, someone was trying to claw themselves free, but only barely managing—a hand fighting to open up a hole between bodies, a head only peeking; knowing it was completely impossible to get out. Always pushing, never coming through.

"And this is me. How I feel, all the time."

It was a human hand that took the painting from her hands and yet Sanja wasn't even surprised. She turned and saw the woman sitting cross legged by her side, keeping track of lines on the canvas with her long, thin fingers, completely mesmerised.

"You like that?" *Do you feel like that too?* she actually wanted to ask.

The mora didn't speak, but Sanja could still feel her answer in the small, caressing movements of her fingertips along the brush strokes; the meticulous way she followed the shapes, like something could abruptly come alive and disappear from sight. It was flattering in a weird way. Not a lot of artists could brag that a supernatural monster was enthralled with their work. Maybe they could, but she didn't know of any instance of it happening.

Sanja used the moment to observe the woman in the golden light of the sun slowly turning in for the evening. She could see the woman's face more clearly now, and it looked familiar but strange, like the face of a neighbour you saw briefly in an elevator, or a parent that came to school once in a year. Her hair was more of a dark brown than black, long and sleek, but not greasy. The white dress she wore reminded Sanja of ugly nightgowns Grandma used to wear—flat, boring and long—not really fashionable. It even showed, almost imperceptible, but still there, the yellow smudges of old age. And on her skin there were bruises. A black eye on her face. White half moon impressions of Sanja's teeth on her arms. In the light of the day, she looked more like an abused lonely woman in a decrepit dress, than a goth girl from horror movies who haunts Sanja's dreams.

Sanja leaned in, but refrained from touching at the last moment. She had the strongest urge to move a lock of the long dark hair behind the woman's ear, the better to see her face, but ultimately didn't want to disturb her. She also didn't want to spook the woman; there was a precarious, but tangible truce currently in effect between them, and she didn't want to risk that. Didn't want a repeat of their previous interaction.

What did she want?

Sanja cleared her throat. "I'm glad someone likes it."

The woman glanced in her direction. It was hard to understand the look in her glassy eyes. It was hard to communicate with someone who was so silent, so unresponsive. But there was a light there, behind the irises.

"I could paint you, too, if you want me to."

Sanja mused over ideas for a moment, while the mora watched her closely. She could see the picture in her mind. On the bottom, she would paint an intangible body of an unnamed woman with a face obscured in darkness. Pressing on the woman would be the mora's body, made in clear strokes with harsh lines. Her face caught in the middle of shapeshifting, unclear. The pose of the two would evoke the images of lovers embracing, violence and eroticism merged together in a hint of torment and sex.

But she couldn't voice that. It was too serious, too real. Too mad. Instead, she joked. "I could paint you sucking on a toe of some poor sucker. But not in that dress. Something more flattering. A vintage look, but with style. Do you think you could pull off a Victorian look?"

Sanja giggled over the thought of the mora in a brocade corset. She was definitely losing her mind. The woman scrunched her eyebrows, looking so much like a cat at the moment that Sanja started to laugh even louder, feeling lighter than before, like silly jokes could erase the heavy thoughts that clouded her brain.

"Sorry, sorry, I'm not making fun of you, I swear. Sorry..." But the damage was already done. The woman disappeared into thin air, and Sanja's painting almost fell on the floor without anyone there to keep holding it, but her reflexes kicked in at the last moment and she caught it.

Her laughter slowly fizzled out after that. What was the point if there was no one there to share her joy? She turned the painting in her hands, remembered how engrossed in it the other woman had been. No one had ever seen this piece before. It was as personal as her dreams.

In the end she hung it in the bedroom, above her bed, like a peace offering.

6

The phone's generic melody rang out in the silence of her apartment for the third time. Holding the cell in sweaty hands, she looked at the display, thinking whether or not it would be smart to ignore it like the last two times. But the missed call notifications were as anxiety inducing as answering, prone to sour her whole day, completely destroying any sort of peace she had and trashing her weekend. No matter what she'd tried to do—watch TV or read a book—there was always a nagging thought in her head, in the shape of an icon of a bent arrow bouncing from the handset.

Knowing that she was merely postponing her inevitable irritation, she answered the third call at the last moment, while putting the last of the dishes in the sink, after her meager lunch.

"Hey, Grandma," she said in greeting, watching the knife drop in the sink. It was dirty with pizza crust, with a little bit of dark red tomato juice on its blade.

"I was trying to get to you the whole day. I made some homemade fig jam, already gave Marija and Shimun some, but there's some left for you, too."

Sanja closed her eyes and took a silent breath, hoping her Grandma won't be able to hear the sigh on the phone. "I was working," she said before remembering it was Saturday, "I had some papers to grade. Didn't hear the phone."

"Listening to you, people would think you're a doctor and not a teacher," came a derisive reply. Grandma's neighbour, after all, had a granddaughter that was a doctor, working in Germany. She came to visit in an expensive looking car, while Sanja drove a beat up Fiat, fifteen years old. Her Grandma liked to point out that fact four out of five times during any conversation.

"Thanks for the offer," Sanja decided to get back to the topic at hand, in hope it'll end the call sooner rather than later, "but I don't need any jam. Especially not fig jam. Remember? I don't like figs." What she didn't say was that she didn't like the taste that reminded her of the beatings. For the same reason her stomach didn't tolerate walnuts, the mere smell of walnut *rakija* making her nauseous.

"It's tasty, this batch is the best one I've ever made. Tastes like heaven. Everybody thinks so. Also, I can't give it to some grandchildren and not others, it wouldn't be fair."

Sanja rubbed her eyes with her free hand, wanting nothing more but to end the call and go to the bed early. Instead, she leaned over the sink, trying to focus on the dirty dishes she had to wash—the piles upon piles of plates and pots, cups with moldy layers of coffee dregs—a small hill she'd made by not really cleaning anything after meals for days.

"It could be a housewarming present."

The lighthearted statement cut her breath like a sucker punch. "What?" She managed to mumble. *What housewarming?* she was afraid to ask, dreading the answer.

"Well, of course it's not the only present. I bought you a real one, a good one, as soon as you told me you'd bought a place. I was foolish enough to think you'll invite me over, show me this new shiny apartment of yours. But here we are, months later, and still nothing. I have to lie to my neighbours that I'd been to your place, that it's big and spacious, with a beautiful view, obviously planned for a family, just so they don't figure out that I haven't been invited yet. I don't even know your address. I'm your grandmother, I was your legal guardian, I took care of you, clothed you and fed you, and yet, in the end, I wasn't even invited to your new home. Not to mention your sporadic visits, it's easier to see the Pope then you. Am I really that undeserving?" She said, while she actually thought: Have I really raised such an ungrateful child? Sanja knew her well, could read, without a doubt, the hidden lines. She could sense rancor in the air, making her almost gag. Wanted nothing more than say to her: *yes, you really are so unworthy and yes, you did raise such a thankless brat. That's all on you.*

But instead she closed her eyes and tried to slow the beating of her heart. "I just don't have a lot of time," she heard herself say. "Didn't have time to clean it all up, make it presentable. I still have some furniture missing." The hollow justifications made her sick to her stomach. Where was that anger that had made her beat up the mora? Where was that strength? She hears Grandma's voice and she's suddenly in the same, closed space where she was left to cry alone; she's again hiding behind the bed from the lashes.

"And yet you had time to get a cat. Don't think your cousins are not speaking to me. A cat? You keep an animal in your home? Cats are supposed to be outside, in the yard, to catch rats. What's happening in this world, has everyone gone mad?"

"It keeps me company."

"You wouldn't need a cat for a company if you had a husband. Do you want to turn into a spinster? Living alone, with a cat! You would do better to find yourself a man. Trust me, it's not as lonely when you can share your life with someone. Sanja, what are you doing with your life?"

The question caught her unprepared. This had to be a nightmare. This was probably just the mora, messing with her head. At any moment, she'll wake up and start breathing normally again. She'll yell at the mora, sure, but at least this horrible conversation would end.

"You have no boyfriend, no husband. The only thing you have is your job and the apartment I've never seen. This is not the way to live. And if you at least had a career to show I could say to my neighbours 'well she's not married because she's a very important person at her very important job, you know how it is with this new generation,' but it's not even that! I thought you were smarter than that."

"I'm happy with my life. I love my job," Sanja lied. And that was the worst part of it. The thing that ate her from the inside, like a poisonous millipede drilling in her intestines. The repugnant lie burned her tongue. Why was she such a failure? Why did she let it get to the point when Grandma was right? What she had was existing, not living. Like an old painting someone had started, but never finished working on.

The mora was the most exciting part of her life, and that was the creature that tried to kill her through nightmares on most nights.

"Are you? Are you really?" Grandma sounded sceptical. "Marija says that she's happy, but look at her. Who can believe her?" And just like that she derailed, finding a new target. It was always like that. Circling the family members with her tongue-lashing. "She's fussing over her son like he's a porcelain doll. He's a boy, he shouldn't be coddled! And yet it's always 'he can't eat this, he can't wear that, he's sensitive, he's special.' Dragging him to a doctor because he had a bad dream and—"

"What?" Her question rang so loud it managed to cut through Grandma's monologue. The world tilted around her; light in the bulb emphasizing her pale arm gripping onto the sink, making it seem unnaturally, bone white and thin. The coppery taste lingered in her mouth, while she remembered that one dream in which she found the mora sucking on her little cousin's toes.

“Yes, that was my reaction too,” Grandma sounded vindicated. “Who goes to the doctor because of a nightmare?”

“Why would she do that?” There must’ve been more to that story, but Sanja wasn’t sure whether she wanted to hear it or not. It probably had nothing to do with her mora, but still, an iron grip of fear closed in on her, made her count her breaths.

“Marija said that he had that... what do they call it... when you wake up in the middle of the night and hallucinate and can’t move?”

“Sleep paralysis?”

“Yeah, that. The boy had a nightmare. Woke up and thought there was someone in the room with him, leaning down on the bed. Couldn’t move out of fear.” At that part, Grandma snorted, showing fully well what she thought of her great grandson. “Freaked out. Marija freaked out too. She made it sound like he has some untreatable sickness. It happened once and yet she was ready to go on a pilgrimage.”

He tastes bitter, the mora told Sanja in that dream, displeased with her meal. She could remember it clearly, which should be impossible. And yet, it stayed with her—her kid cousin lay on the bed, soundlessly sleeping, while the mora knelt and sucked on his toe like it was a treat. Was it truly possible that she’d dreamed of something that actually happened? While it was happening?

She couldn’t grasp the meaning of that, too afraid to contemplate. It was supposed to be her cross to bear. And yet, it appeared that the mora visited someone else. And not just anyone, but her family. A kid. Did Shimun know that? Has he made a connection? Were they all in danger because of her?

No. If he did, he would already be at her door with holy water and more reprimands up his sleeve, but he hasn’t shown his face ever since their last fight. And if Grandma was right, it had only happened once.

"What did the doctor say?" she managed to ask, feeling nauseous. That pizza she ate might end up finding its way out from her digestive system and, if that happened, it wouldn't look good on her kitchen floor.

"Oh, nothing much. That he needs to improve his sleeping habits. Something about the way the kid's playing games all night on his phone instead of sleeping isn't healthy. Who would have thought that, huh? When I say that, I'm a harpy, but when the doctor says it, then it's a commandment to be followed."

A movement at the periphery drew her attention away from Grandma's voice. The mora, wearing her human shape, came into the living room and started watching her with care. Did she know what the conversation was about? She didn't look worried, but why would she be? It wasn't like she cared what Sanja thought about her. It wasn't as if Sanja didn't know what she was.

"...and really, it's all because Marija's husband is absentent for months, out at sea, so that child doesn't have a good role model and–"

"Hey, Grandma," she cut through, not interested in listening to this kind of talk. The mora sat on the couch, all proper like, with hands on her knees and her back straight; as if she was waiting for Sanja's judgement. "I'm sorry, but I have to go."

"What? Where? Don't you dare cut me off." Grandma's voice was laced with threat in the shape of a good ol' branch.

Sanja's breath hitched; for a moment she was in the dark again. This time, though, she decided to brace it. She wasn't alone. The woman that had tried to strangle her—quite literally—was full of bruises Sanja had left. There was strength in her. She didn't need to dance to Grandma's tune.

“I have a life, you know. Even if you don’t believe it. So, if you’ll excuse me, but I gotta go now.” Before Grandma could butt in with the reply, Sanja hung up. She felt a strange calm, but also foreboding, fully aware this won’t end up well. Grandma will find a way to have her word be the last.

But right now, she had another problem to deal with. The one who was currently watching her with big doe eyes.

“Do you know what we were talking about?”

Sanja was surprised by how placid she sounded. How still she was. No matter how hard she tried to make herself feel something tangible—disgust, anger, fear—it was all dulled, like a blunt blade of an old knife.

“Did you attack Dario, that little kid who visited me the other day?” She wasn’t even sure why she bothered to ask. It wasn’t like the mora would answer her. But something curious happened. The mora looked her straight in the eye and nodded her head. Simple as that.

Yes.

“Why?” It was a foolish question, which she knew even without mora’s brow furrowing in confusion. For the same reason Sanja baked the frozen pizza in the oven and then ate it for dinner. She was hungry. Dario was a meal. “I guess you’re unhappy with him?”

The mora shrugged and turned her gaze towards the window. Sanja moved closer, finally finding the will to walk towards the other woman. Any minute now she will know what to do. How to feel.

But the moments passed. Sanja came to a stop in a picture in reverse; the mora sitting down, while Sanja stood over her with closed fists, confused with jumbled thoughts. The mora wasn’t her pet. She wasn’t her friend. And yet she was constantly acting like it.

“I wish you could speak to me. Or, maybe, I wish you wanted to try and find a way to communicate with me. This is frustrating.” Maybe, then it would be easier to have a fight. The mora moved her head again, her eyes blurry with a slight white film over them, but fixed on Sanja. Was she imagining the curiosity there? "I don't know why you're here. With me. Why aren't you haunting someone else? You can obviously move from the apartment, so—why me?"

The mora's eyes were a bottomless pit of a night sky covered in clouds. They pulsed with a rhythm of their own, like lungs expanding and collapsing in their breath cycle. If Sanja continued watching them she would lose the ground below her, lose all of her weight, until she was nothing but an ethereal creature stripped from the heaviness of an organic body.

"Will I become you?" She could hear herself ask. Didn't even know it worried her so much until she finally voiced it.

The mora shrugged, but her eyes were downcast. So it was a maybe.

Great. "Okay. Okay. I don't know what to do with that information." The same way she didn't know anything else. She took a deep breath, turned her back on the mora and went to her liquor cabinet. "I really hope you won't go after my family. At least, if you want to go after someone, go and eat my Grandma. She's old, she's already lived enough, not to mention that she's kind of mean. Probably won't be a good meal, but if someone deserves nightmares it's her."

The image of the mora sucking on Grandma's old corn riddled toes wasn't the sort of thing she wanted in her head. And yet it showed up uninvited, making her shudder in disgust. "I just wish..." She stopped at the wooden doors, unable to look at the mora's face. Not wanting to see the answer in them. Not knowing what she'll do if she was truly on the path to become a mora as well. A part of her just wanted to let it all play out, or to worry about that tomorrow. Another part was angry that she'd made so little effort to learn what she was dealing with. "I just wish I could understand you. I wish we could be friends." It was the truth. The mora already knew her deepest fears, her true nightmares, and she was a wretched soul herself. There would be no judgment from her. Sanja wouldn't need to be perfect, wouldn't need to be careful with her words and actions. Maybe her life wouldn't be as empty if there could be companionship between them.

It was a foolish thought, and when she turned again—with a bottle of Teacher's whisky in her hand—the mora wasn't there anymore and she was alone again.

* * *

A small pressure on her back woke Sanja up from dreamless slumber.

She was drowsing, slowly falling in and out of darkness, lying on her stomach, with one hand under the pillow. She was aware—somewhere in the back of her head—that her circulation was blocked and, soon, all feeling in her hand would die off, forcing her to wake up truly, in anguish. Still, she'd apparently managed to fall asleep like that, because at one point there was blessed nothingness, and at the other she was brought back to consciousness; to her nose burrowed deep in the stained pillow, the weight on her arm, the utter darkness, and a long, slender body, caressingly moving against her back.

So, we're back at the games. A disappointing thought, if not unexpected. It wasn't like before, though. The mora wasn't pushing at her chest, wasn't trying to choke her. Instead, her movements were like a massage; the thick body ever so slightly touching Sanja, moving against her length, slithering upward from her feet towards her head.

Even through the near darkness it wasn't hard to discern the body of a snake. Sanja moved her head a little, enough to see small red eyes looking at her, illuminated in the dark. Sometime during the night, the duvet had fallen from Sanja's body to the floor, but, with the night being unusually warm, she didn't even notice. Now she was aware that there was nothing between her pajamas and a gigantic fucking snake, whose weight enveloped her like a reptilian blanket.

It made a small hissing sound and Sanja felt the wet sensation of a forked tongue lightly touching her chin. Sanja held her breath, unsure what to do. A realistic part of her brain screamed danger, reminding her that snakes were perfectly shaped to suffocate their prey, but the other part of her, a stupid, curious, morbid part, wanted to know what the mora will do next. It felt like they were finally getting somewhere, moving away from the usual nightmares and strangulation, but what if she was wrong? What if she was just imagining that the mora wanted to do something other than to feed on Sanja while she slept? Maybe she was just projecting, and when the snake started to squeeze her breath away, her heart will break from being such a naive girl.

Slowly, trying not to disturb the animal on her, she fully turned to lie on her back and the snake shifted with her, but didn't constrict. Sanja could still breathe, her throat unobstructed.

"Do what you need to do," Sanja whispered in the night and closed her eyes.

A small bite quickly stung at her neck, as fast as a wave hitting the shore on a stormy night, piercing her skin like a needle in the vein. Cold hunger tingled in the pit of her stomach; her limbs went impossibly heavy, filled with molten iron. Centipedes on fire—hundreds of them—marched all over her skin, jabbing thousands of tiny fiery legs into her like miniature stilettos, everywhere they went. They managed to slip through her ears, going all the way to her brain, igniting it.

A sensation of floating in the air; her burning body sailing until there was nothing left of her world but a rippling reflection on a grainy background, like she was suddenly stuck in an old black and white movie.

Two young women screeched in happiness, running among fluffy white lambs and sheep, but Sanja could hear their laughter only as a broken up audio. Their faces were lost in the past, like a picture faded with age, and yet it could be easy to mistake one of them for her mora. The girl's sleek dark hair danced in the air, unbound, and her eyes were brown pearls instead of dark glass. Her chest moved up and down with breaths, but still, *still*, there was something there that screamed to Sanja with its familiarity. The face of her nightmares.

The other girl, though, that one Sanja never seen before, but her features spelled *love*. It wasn't important who she was or how she looked, whether her face was heart-shaped or oval, whether her hair was brown or blond or black. The only thing that mattered was the way the other girl felt. Like the sun after the rain bringing out the rainbow, the smell of a freshly baked bread to a hungry stomach. She was love personified, and she danced with the maybe-mora in the bright green pastures and they smiled and they kissed and they made love.

The world lost its balance and Sanja slipped, falling in the weightless tar, until it cleared in front of her eyes. The girl that could be mora knelt on the corn, her eyes forlorn, inhaling the chalk dust. Tears slowly dripped from her eyes, but no sound escaped her mouth. She was as still as a statue of the Virgin Mary, as calm as a dead clam on the bottom of the sea. A faceless man stood over her, only a pink gnarled hole for his mouth. The noise he made was a wave, shaking the woman on the corn to her core. Sanja couldn't understand what he was saying, but she could taste the acidic poison of his words.

Then the corn below the woman's knees shifted, turning into the solid brown of a bench. But the woman stayed in the same position, her face downcast under the watchful gaze of a mangled priest. His features were hidden behind the translucent lacy veil like a blushing bride, except yellow pus poured down his chin while he spoke at the altar, his hands outstretched toward his congregation. The infection leaked with every word, and the stream slowly reached the kneeling woman, grabbing for her legs, moving toward her head. She moved her head only slightly, but otherwise didn't react. Just absorbed the festering pus disappearing inside her ear, until nothing was left of the discharge.

Again the scene shifted, causing vertigo. Sanja's vision was now spinning uncontrollably, and in the turmoil she caught a glimpse of the two young women and a new man, on the backdrop of a looming church. Focusing on the trio helped her sight clear and brought her weightless body closer to them. Both of the women were, indeed, from the earlier vision, but their posture was drastically different. There was no laughter, no running free, no kissing under the sun. The girl with long sleek hair and brown eyes had an empty look, hiding hate and despair inside her. The other one, the one whose features Sanja couldn't define no matter how hard she tried, stood in the embrace of a man with eight eyes on his face and a tongue dangling from the pit of his mouth. His arms were long and sharp ended, one of which was draped over the woman with feigned nonchalance. There was a sad smile on the woman's face, a golden band on her finger and a cross on a necklace, shining brightly against her skin, dazzling Sanja. The woman tried to say she's sorry with her eyes—*you know how it is*; *we can't*; *that life is not for us*—while saliva kept dripping from the man's tongue on her collarbone, sliding down towards her breasts.

The brown eyed woman stretched her mouth into an impossibly large hole and screamed. The radio in Sanja's ears ruptured from the fierceness of the sound, but it couldn't compare to the hollow feeling in her heart. The scream started sucking in flies, the ground, the woman with the golden ring and the eight-eyed man and, in the end the whole sun above, until there was nothing more to take inside. Until she started choking on the things she'd inhaled. The woman put her hands against her neck in panic, trying to breathe, tears falling from her eyes without reserve while her whole body shaked. Her eyes pleaded for help, but Sanja couldn't move from her place of a spectator to someone else's pain, a silent watcher of a slow suffocating. And then the world went dark.

When it came back, it was in the grey of a perpetual dawn, except it would never be day again without a sun to shine in the sky. And there was the dark-haired woman now, older, walking on concrete among ugly, grey skyscrapers, with her city clothes and her empty mask and shallow breaths. Never again would she take a deep breath. Not in this place of desolation—a soulless town for a tired woman who walked with a seed of a shadow at her heels. Her legs dragged her through a world constantly moving like a fast train, elusive, and she would sit and write and eat with dark circles under her eyes, completely drained from willpower and strength. Her dreams of love—only a thing of the past. And if she wasn't alone at home, she was surrounded with heaps of the little ones, children with colorful glassy beads instead of eyes whose grabby fingers tried to steal parts of the woman, her meat, her hair, her brain, everything she could give them, and then even those things she could not. And the more they took the more dead inside she was, disappearing until almost nothing was left of her except her hunger.

It couldn't be filled, couldn't be met. She could open her sharp mouth and eat the children alive, but it wouldn't fill the pit in her stomach. And oh, how she turned her ire on them, giving them cold cruelty instead of the corn for kneeling of her youth, finding ways to bite into their souls, grab the insides of their dreams and shred them into bloody ribbons. But she still couldn't satisfy the hole in her heart and that knowledge turned her sour and angry. Bitterness and loneliness dripped from her sweat and fed the shadowy hunger at her heels. With time, her body became shrunken and wrinkled like dry fruit, while the shadow started growing taller and fuller in its shape. But it wasn't until the woman died, alone in her bed, without a person in the world who would care, that the shadow finally snapped free.

It took the shape of a distorted picture of the woman, dead in the bed, what she looked like when she was younger, before she'd lost her breath to the choking screams. And the shadow screamed over the corpse tucked in the sheets, but there was no sound to accompany its wail.

Sanja blinked, and for a moment she almost didn't recognize her own body, lying in that same bed. How could she? It wasn't the dead old woman anymore, but a lump of condensed light from the long lost sun. It made the shadow irrationally angry, to the point it wanted to destroy it. That feeling was so strong it bled through to Sanja and she almost cheered for the mora as she was trying to smother the light before remembering that it was *her*.

She watched how the mora choked her, tried to devour her, all without much luck. Instead, the nightmares that had bled from Sanja's breath started eating at the mora in turn. Instead, she'd fought back. It was all wrong, even such a young mora knew it was not the way it was supposed to be, and yet she couldn't run away. She should've gone far, found a new victim to haunt. Except it wasn't how it worked, and she found herself tethered to the one girl that she couldn't eat in the world full of buffets. So she stuck around, drawn to that strange woman she was trying to hurt but whose nightmares were a scalding poison that was slowly killing her in return; but who also found new ways to surprise her in a world that lost its appeal. When the hunger got too unbearable, she would try to quench it with the girl and then ask for forgiveness, but Sanja's fire only burned her. So sometimes she slipped away, just to steal a snack somewhere else, ate a morsel here and there where she felt like she could get away with that. But she always came back, not really knowing what she should do with her life or this burning luminous girl that slept in her old room.

* * *

Waking up felt like a slow descent into her body after being cut from it. Her skin was itching in places, but it didn't hurt. There was actually nothing wrong with her body, for once. Her chest normally rose and fell with breaths, and even the snake bite on her neck was only a shallow wound. And yet, inside her lungs, a great lump of unshed tears had accumulated, a river overflowing with spring rain. It was worse than anything she'd felt before, and it wasn't hers. It was only a memory of a dream, a dead woman's phantom pain.

A hand touched her tenderly over her heart. She didn't have to move her head to see that it was the mora, lying beside her in bed. Sanja felt her presence, transformed from snake to human again. Sanja's collarbone felt the cold of the ice under the mora's touch, but it wasn't uncomfortable. In fact, the cooling feeling grounded her, helped with the burning storm of feelings—loneliness, anguish and despair—like a balm.

"Okay, it's okay," she whispered in the dark, through tears that were soundlessly sliding down her cheeks, soaking the pillow below her head. Uncertain for whom that was intended. For her? For the mora? For the old, dead teacher whose apartment she'd bought?

She knew that the woman didn't have kids who could inherit the place. No close kin, only some distant cousin somewhere in the world, who didn't really care. Sanja had never wondered why it was like that, just dumped the old stuff in the trash. Thought the woman's husband might have died before her. Now she knew there were no husbands, no partners, no friends. There was no one, after the girl from her youth, and she'd left with someone else. A man.

Sanja closed her eyes, not even trying to stop the tears for the woman whose grave no one visited. The dreams didn't give her the clearest picture, and she definitely didn't see the woman's whole life like some straightforward movie, but the feelings that leaked from the mora to Sanja were more than familiar. The self inflicted isolation. The pain mixed with anger. The hunger for something that, in time, turns to a hunger for everything.

She'd died alone in her bed. And Sanja wasn't sure whether her spirit had become the mora, or if the woman had willed her to life with her scorn and bitterness. Wasn't even important anymore. The woman was dead, and in her place only the mora remained.

"We don't need to be enemies. Don't you see? You don't need to be alone anymore. We don't need to be alone."

Sanja put her open palm over the mora's hand that was still on her chest. Kept her like that, in place, while she breathed. Letting the woman feel her breaths when she couldn't inhale herself anymore. And mourned for a woman she'd never met and whose life could have easily been her own.

7

After a few days of peaceful sleep at night, Sanja came well rested to the church smelling of burning candles and wax, wood and incense. It instantly brought her back to Sunday mornings spent sitting on an uncomfortable bench, stubbornly silent, while dozens around her prayed. Sometimes, her Grandma would notice her refusal to participate in mass, and those days were among the worse ones.

In the present, the son of God followed her with his marble eyes from his place of eternal crucifixion, fixed on the wall, while she silently walked toward Shimun. Her cousin had his back turned to her, putting fresh flowers—white and purple lilies—in front of a Virgin Mary statue on a side altar at the apse.

“Forgive me father, for I have sinned,” she whispered, breathing down his neck.

“Sanja?!” Shimun made an undignified sound she could only guess was her name. His voice echoed in the emptiness of church. He was also, Sanja noticed, looking like he was on the verge of jumping out of his own skin and joining the saints in Heaven. In the process, he’d almost punched her in the face with his flailing elbow.

“Don’t you have someone else to do this instead of you? You have those old ladies that clean and take care of the church. Are they on vacation?”

Shimun took a moment to compose himself, with a hand of his vest. "Dead God, Sanja, I almost had a heart attack."

"Sorry," she said, but felt too much like smiling to actually mean it.

"Yeah, I see how regretful you are." Despite it, his voice turned lighthearted. "And to answer your question, I actually like to bring out the flowers from our garden, usually after a walk. How did you know I was here anyway?"

"Your boss, and I don't mean the big one in the sky, but the human one in a black dress, told me I could find you here. By the way, did you know he talks to himself while strolling in the courtyard?"

"He's not... he's probably praying. Rosary. Remember that?"

"Didn't see any beads in his hands, though."

Shimun sighed and rolled his eyes, forever looking like a martyr when talking to her. But there was something else there, too, in his face, mixed with a light smile, blurred like water full of chlorine, painting him with awkwardness. So, her jokes weren't good enough to mend the broken bridges between them.

Sanja put her right hand over her bruised chest, where the mora's light touch still lingered, even in broad daylight. "Look, can we go somewhere to talk?"

Both sets of smiles twinkled out, replaced by seriousness. Sanja could feel the memory of their fight still lingering between them, a heavy weight on her chest. He nodded his head.

"Yeah, come on. I'll make us a cup of coffee."

The crucified Christ followed her out with his dark sunken eyes, blood from his crown of thorns dripping down. His piercing judgment stuck between her shoulder blades until she blessedly got out of the church and far away from his damaging look.

The kitchen was small and cozy, designed to fit maybe three people max. With a miniature stove, sink, fridge, table and liquor cabinet, and a gigantic painting of Saint Don Bosco—whose head looked like it was stung by hornets. Sanja had never been here before, didn't even expect that one of the rooms adjacent to the nave would be something so mundane. For some reason she forgot that her cousin had a normal life inside of the church, like she'd half expected the priests to simply spawn for the mass like in a video game.

There was an old looking coppery cezve on the stove—probably older than Shimun and her combined—and he filled it with water. Everything was ancient there, Sanja noticed, with a smell of deterioration and a worn up look. Decrepit. Even her cousin, at only thirty years old, already felt like a dried out shell of a young man, just by standing there. If she looked closely, would she see that his skin was nothing but a mummified membrane conserved by the will of a killed God?

He turned towards her and indicated the liquor cabinet with his hand. "Do you want—"

"No, I'm okay," she interrupted him and sat at the table, feeling too out of place in this strange room that still didn't really exist in her head. She turned her back to Saint Don Bosco and his busted face; some sort of joke about finding a better artist worthy of the saints lingered on the surface of her tongue, but in the end she squashed it. She came to apologize and to bury the axe, not to insult decorations of Shimun's place of work. "So... I'm sorry for kicking you out of my apartment. I mean, I'm still a little angry at you for some of the things you said to me, especially stuff about my dad, but I should have handled it better. You are like a brother to me, I hope you know that. I don't like this distance, this empty space, between us. And I know you only tried to help me with the mora."

For a few moments, the only thing that could be heard was boiling water, while Shimun leaned against the sink, watching her with immense attention. Knowing how alike they are, their eyes almost the same color and shape, she wondered if this is what she looked like to others in moments of great inside turmoil.

"I... Jesus Sanja, it's me who's sorry. I really, really am. I was an asshole, and honestly, I wanted to see you and apologise to you ages ago, but I wasn't certain if you'd want to have anything to do with me. I was a coward and it should've been me asking for your forgiveness, not the other way around." He sounded anguished in a way she'd never heard him speak before, and it soothed her anger better than his apology.

On the verge of tears, he turned his back to her, with the excuse of making them coffee. She let him have his dignity and waited patiently for the practised moves, until he could show her his face again.

A few moments later, he put the little ceramic cup, full with steaming black coffee, in front of her. The smell—tangible and real—calmed her nerves and she brought it under her nose and inhaled.

"Thanks," she said. "Not just for the coffee."

He shrugged, still skittish. It was probably because the small golden crucified Jesus dangled from his neck, weighing him down. A slow strangulation he wasn't even aware of. How did she not notice this before?

"I'm not going to try to speak over you now. I don't... I don't necessarily understand your stubbornness regarding that thing at your place. But I should've known better then to say that stuff about your dad. It's just, to be honest..." he sighed and sat in front of her with his own cup between his palms. "Sometimes, I too get angry at my uncle. I shouldn't, and I know you'll get angry at me for saying that, but it doesn't change the fact that he hurt you with what he's done. You and your mom. And maybe she'd be alive still if he found a way to deal with his pain that didn't involve taking his own life. I'm sorry. But every time I see you missing them, every time I see you miserable with Grandma, I get a little bit angrier at him." After that confession he closed his eyes and braced himself like he was ready for her to throw the scalding coffee on his face. And maybe if they'd had this conversation at some other time, when she was too wired, she would've been sorely tempted to do that. But now she was too tired to fight. And besides, she could understand how he felt. "You know, I was never angry at him. I think I poured all of that emotion towards Grandma," *not that she didn't deserve that*, she thought, but decided to keep that to herself, "and there were times when I simply thought it must've been something I did or something I lacked. Because I wasn't enough for him to stick around." Her voice wavered for a bit. "Our Grandma used to say to my mom that she hadn't been good enough, or else he wouldn't have wanted to die. So I probably internalised some of it. But after mom's death, I didn't think a lot about him. Didn't want to, I guess. It's probably why that dream about him left me feeling so raw." A dream, or simply an image of him standing in front of her, alive and old. Reminding her of what she'd lost. "It doesn't matter now. He wasn't even the topic of our conversation. If I remember correctly, you were worried about me dying in my bed. Or about my soul ending in Hell."

Shimun sighed and leaned back on his chair. The sun behind him illuminated his hair through the window, crowning him with a halo. It hurt her eyes, but she didn't look away. "How could I not be worried? There's a literal demon hanging over you. You said I was like a brother to you. Well, you are my little sister more so than my flesh and blood half-siblings; the one that's been the longest with me. I don't want to officiate your funeral. I'm the older one, I'm going in the ground first, you understand?"

"I don't think I like that. I already had to bury my parents, why would I want to have to outlive you too?"

"Well, tough. Older people get to go first. And I want you there at my deathbed, all wrinkled and hunched over, supported by some younger wife and your kids. Understood?"

Sanja shook her head and felt tears welling inside her eyes, even when she must've already cried out all of her soul the night before. How could he say it so simply, like having someone who could love her for life was possible for her?

"I would like to say that we don't need to think about that because we're still young and have our whole life ahead of us," she offered "But that's not true, is it? Or at least, we can't know that for sure. Just ask my parents. Or even grandpa. He certainly didn't expect cancer. But, I think you don't need to be afraid of me getting eaten by the mora."

His eyes wandered all over her face, like they were trying to detect a lie. Or like there was a way for him to get inside her mind and look around in there. And she briefly wondered, how many people would he find lurking inside?

"Look, I know it's hard to understand, I know what it looks like. Me... just... living there with a mora like it were a ficus. And my behavior isn't the healthiest, either. But the mora actually isn't even at fault for that." He looked incredulous, and she hurried to explain. "I've been thinking. This whole situation has just shown me something important that I've been ignoring on purpose. And that's the fact that I've stopped living. At some point I just started letting stuff happen to me instead of actively trying to live my life. The last things I proactively did were securing a job and getting a flat, and after that it was like my brain decided it was too tired and took a nap from which I've still not woken up. But I've started to stir up." Her next breath filled all of her lungs with air. "I've started waking up. And the biggest irony is that it was the mora's nightmares that played a crucial role in that."

"While I'm... I guess, glad that you got to some important revelations, I don't understand how you can be so sure that mora won't try to kill you, or succeed at it. And even if she's not actively hurting you, having troubles with sleeping can't really be helpful for your health."

"And that's a sensible question, one I'm not sure how to answer. But, I need you to trust me," she reached out to him and he took her palms in his. "This isn't me deciding to leave my life to just unravel, without my input or design. Even if it looks like I just want to die, it's not that. I'm not suicidal. I've found a way to live with the mora. My own way. Now I just need to figure out how to deal with the rest." The rest being her life; everything entangled in that one word. The loneliness. The anxiety. The pain. In the end, the mora turned out to be the simplest problem to solve, an outside threat. While Sanja felt inside as if she were a house drowning in trash, with no idea about where to start with cleanup.

But there was a simple first step she could take, after all, and it involved a certain number saved on her phone. She didn't believe she would ever seek professional help, but after her visit to the mora's nightmares she was certain of one thing. That sort of life wasn't something she ever wanted to experience in the waking world. Nor did she want to turn into her grandmother, unfeeling, closed up and cruel.

"Okay, I trust you," Shimun conceded, shocking her with how easily he'd given up. And he must've seen it in her face because he added,"No, I really do. I know *you*. You were always tougher than any of us. I was just worried you didn't want to deal with the mora, that you'd rather let her do to you whatever she felt like doing."

"And I know we don't see eye to eye regarding Grandma... I know it feels like I'm always on her side, but I just don't know how else to... how..."

To deal with the fact that the person who shaped all of your life is a bad guy, Sanja supplemented in her head, but didn't say out loud. He didn't need more lashes from her, even the imaginary ones that her words could bring. His God was doing enough flagellation for her to need to jump in. "I know. Just... when I'm ranting about her, can you not jump to her defence?"

"It's really a knee jerk reaction at this point," he nervously laughed. "But you're right, I should just shut up and listen to what you have to say. Is there... is there a way I could make it up to you for acting like such a douche?"

"Well, since you asked..." Her visit here wasn't just to smooth out their fight. She also came with a secret agenda, one on which she'd sat until it felt was the right time to bring it up. She grabbed her bag. "There's a huge favour I need to ask of you."

Even though her voice sounded grave, he didn't look alarmed. Instead, there was a solid severity on his face—the official priest's face. She slid towards him a small piece of paper, a name written on it in blue ink.

"This is the woman who lived in my apartment before me." Or at least she hoped she had it right. She had to walk three stories down before finding a flat with an old woman who'd lived there since the building was finished and still remembered other original tenants. Still, she couldn't actually be certain whether the woman's memory was correct. "Can you find out where she's buried? I know the Church has records of stuff like christenings, weddings and funerals. I don't know who the priest was that officiated at her funeral, but I'm pretty sure there must've been one."

"That's quite a big job. Do you know when she died?" At least he didn't ask what she needed it for. Even though she could guess that he would, sooner or later.

"Will the year be enough? I don't have the exact date, but I can pinpoint the time of year." If the realtor who showed her the apartment had been truthful. The uncertainties piled up so high that she wasn't hopeful Shimun would be able to find what she was looking for, but she had to try. Better than trying to contact some stranger and explaining to him why she wanted to visit the grave of a distant cousin he didn't really care about. If he even knew where she was buried.

"Well, this is certainly a challenge. I'll start with our parish and then ask around. Can't promise anything, but I'll try my best."

"And that's all I'm asking for."

She smiled, feeling like she was finally on the right track with her life.

* * *

The grave was neglected; covered in cypress tree needles and dirt. It was at the end of the row, and the only one that didn't have any sort of candles or flowers on it. Not even the dead, wilted ones that would show that once upon a time someone had visited the grave. A sad sigh escaped Sanja's mouth, but she wasn't really surprised.

In the end, Shimun didn't have a lot of trouble tracking it down. After eliminating his own parish, he decided to check with the next logical possibility. Every parish had its own territory—streets and buildings that fell under its care—so he simply went to the one that had her building's tenants in its congregation. Of course, if the woman had wanted to be a part of another parish in life, it wouldn't have been as easy. Or if she'd simply stopped going to church. Sanja wondered why she'd continued to be part of the institution that had hurt her so much, if she even interpreted the mora's dream with the priest leaking pus correctly.

Shimun had even learned a bit about the old woman from her priest, but nothing new, not to Sanja at least. Simply how she was a lonely woman that kept to the side, came to mass, went through the motions, but had no friends to stick around after with, showed no real interest in being a part of the community. She'd bought herself a grave plot at some point, apparently not wanting to be buried in her family's grave, somewhere in some island village from which she hailed. Sanja couldn't blame her for that. She hadn't seen her whole life in that dream, but she could guess a thing or two, given the time in which the woman had lived. Sanja wouldn't want to share her last space on Earth with her Grandma either.

The headstone was plain, with nothing but the barest information. The name, the dates—birth and death—otherwise empty. There was no personalised message, not even a song lyric or a Bible verse. She'd bought herself a tomb, but probably hadn't thought about preparing the headstone. What would've she written if she had? *I was dead for years before lying down for all eternity.* Or maybe it would be more like: *Beware, because I'm sticking around.*

Sanja shook her head and went to work. She lowered the big bags she'd brought with her on the ground, and took out a small brush first. Methodically and without a thought, she mopped out the needles and dirt. When she was satisfied with how clean it was, she took out the flowers—chrysanthemums—a little worse for the wear after being stuck in the bag. The bouquet was still quite lush, though, and she put it in a container she'd bought for this purpose alone and filled it with water. In the end, she lit the candle, the only one that didn't have any sort of religious symbols on it that she was able to find at the store.

"There," she said to the grave. Even with Sanja's flowers and the candle, it still looked abandoned in comparison with the adjacent one, bursting like a flower shop with all that it held. But it wasn't as bad as before. So she hoped her intention counts as something.

"You know, I'm not going to act like I know you. It would be an easy mistake to make. I can assume things. I can even relate to some of them. And I know that I'd only glimpsed the surface of your life. I know you were more than the mora you've left behind you. But she's the only version of you that I got to meet so I hope you're not angry with me for mourning you even though I never even knew you."

She wasn't even doing this to placate the mora. She, in fact, hadn't even bothered Sanja with nightmares ever since that night. Sanja wasn't able to feel her presence for days, before finally catching her in the form of the cat, sitting in front of a newly started acrylic painting—it was still unclear what it was supposed to be, but there was a vague woman's shape on it—in the studio. Giddy with unexplained joy that the mora didn't abandon her, Sanja had sat close to the cat and started petting her. The cat had purred in a show of content, looking pleased, happy and full. They'd sat like that and watched the painting until the mora stood up and disappeared like she usually didi.

So, this wasn't really for the mora to feel better, if something like that was even possible. Not even for Sanja's own peace. Maybe she was acting foolish, but she couldn't bear the thought that no one remembered the old woman. That the world had forgotten her as soon as she wasn't breathing anymore. Discarded, like her life had meant nothing, after she wasn't even able to find her place in society.

Just an empty stone amidst a row of elaborate headstones.

* * *

A loud, shrieking sound jerked her from her melancholic thoughts and she bent down towards the bags to retrieve her phone. In the silence of the graveyard the ringtone felt disgraceful, a violent blemish on the quiet perfection.

"Yes?" she answered, wondering why Shimun was calling her.

"Sanja," his voice was so hollow that she gripped the phone in her hand. "Sanja..." he repeated her name, like it was the only word he had left.

"Shimun, what's wrong? Are you all right, did something happen?" Maybe he got into an accident. Or he found the old priest, who led his parish dead in the courtyard with scattered rosary beads in his hands. Or maybe–

"Grandma's dead," he finally said.

Sanja lost feeling in her legs. She sat on the grave. It was a good thing she'd cleaned it earlier.

"What?" The word was heavy on her tongue. Her thoughts sluggish. Not really understanding what her cousin was saying.

"Grandma..." And his voice finally broke into tears, drowning any words he could be trying to say.

"Shimun, Shimun please, you're scaring me," she tried. Still peculiarly disconnected from her own voice, her own body, her own thoughts. Like someone who was standing aside and watching the play in front of their eyes.

She could hear Shimun sobbing on the other side of the line, completely wrecked. Her hand still gripped the phone hard, the only thing that felt tangible, real, in a world that suddenly didn't make sense.

The sounds of rustling and then someone else was speaking in her ear. "Hey, it's Marija," her other cousin took over the phone. "I'm sorry, he insisted on calling you himself, but he's a mess."

"Marija, thank God." Her other cousin sounded composed, calm, so whatever happened couldn't have been that bad. "For fuck sakes, what's going on? Shimun is freaking me out!"

"Grandma's dead. I found her in her bed this morning. Came to visit her, she didn't answer the door so I let myself in and... God I'm so stupid, I should've let my mom check her, I don't need this sort of image haunting me."

"What, how?" This shouldn't be possible. Not their Grandma–the woman would outlive them all just out of spite. Just so she could stand on their graves and spit out how worthless they all had been before dying. Not her Grandma, who'd buried her own young daughter and son-in-law, and still stood strong and tough like a mountain. Sanja must've been hearing that wrong. She couldn't be dead.

"Yeah, so, I called the ambulance and asked Shimun to come, didn't know what else to do—"

"That's not what I'm asking."

"Jesus, Sanja, I'm getting to that. Sorry if my story is not coherent enough for you. Do you know what image will forever be stuck in my brain? No, you can't know, because you haven't visited her for months. Ugh. Anyway, to *answer* your question, it appears she dropped dead in her sleep. Not peaceful, mind you; the coroner says it was probably a heart attack. But can't be sure until he checks properly."

"So how does he know it wasn't peaceful if it was in her sleep?"

"Well, gee, I think the absolutely anguished expression on her face was a good hint. The other one was the fact her hand was grabbing at her chest when she died."

Something popped inside Sanja's brain and suddenly all sorts of emotions hit her body at once in an overwhelming wave. A memory played in her mind's eye. *If you want to go after someone, go and eat my Grandma.* It wasn't even that long ago that she'd said that. The mora had listened to her. She'd gone and given her grandmother such a nightmare that her heart was unable to withstand it. Did it explode in her chest? Will they open her up only to find charred remains of an organ that was already rotten to the core?

Marija continued talking on the phone, but Sanja couldn't hear it over the sound of her own thoughts whirring in her ears. "Marija, I'm going to have you call you later," she managed to spit out and hang up before her cousin could react.

As soon as she did, a loud laughter burst from her chest, uncontrolled and wild, mixed with the tears that were freely falling from her eyes. It was as if every possible emotion tried to get out at the same time. The sadness, the denial, the wrecking guilt, the delight. It all came to her and tried to possess her at the same time, turning her body into a shaking, laughing mess. But she didn't care. She laughed and she cried and she found out she truly and deeply didn't care about what she looked like to the passersby.

And when there were no new tears for her to shed, when all of the laughter was sucked from her lungs, she took a deep breath.

Exhaled.

Wiped at her face with her sleeve to look presentable again. There would be a lot of work. Thankfully, it wasn't her responsibility. Grandma had three living children to take care of her corpse. But Shimun will surely need her to comfort him, unless he puts two and two together and figures out Sanja's involvement in their Grandma's death. *It wasn't my fault, I didn't know the mora would listen to me.* But that was a moot point, wasn't it? *I still willed it, still said it out loud to the mora.*

And yet, she couldn't stop feeling like she'd avenged her mother. She just had to make sure that Shimun doesn't suspect a thing. That was a problem for tomorrow. Today, she was free for the first time in forever, and sure felt like celebrating.

The new painting she was working on will need more golden color, so maybe she can start by going to the art shop. Then she could call Ana and finally ask her if she's available for another date. Maybe even a real one this time. If nothing else, she wanted to tell her about her approaching appointment with a therapist, the one she'd made yesterday, and thank her for giving her the idea to do that in the first place.

With a plan formulating in her head, Sanja stood up from the grave of a woman she'd never met but whose living nightmare she got to experience. And left her with a promise to come back, with an even bigger and fancier bouquet.

Sanja breathed in the air full of sun, promise of life, and the smell of wax and cypress.

Breathed out with nothing but lightness in her chest.

AUTHOR'S NOTES

There's a creature in the Slavic folklore named *mora* or *mare* (in English) that does pretty much what I wrote in here. The mora shows up in the form of a woman, cat, snake or a horse, brings nightmares and tries to strangle the sleeper while sucking out their energy. That's why it's often related to the demons—succubi and incubi—and yes, suckling on toes comes directly from the Istrian (Croatian region) folk tales about moras.

The book Sanja reads actually exists. It's called *Vile s Učke* (*Fairies from the Učka Mountain*) by Evelina Rudan, and it was a huge inspiration for this story. Still, I gave moras my own twist, because not only did I find them just quite interesting, but also because I find the description of them choking their victims similar to my own experience with social anxiety and panic attacks. Not the same thing, of course—the mora is, after all, probably a supernatural explanation of sleep paralysis—but that's where my brain went. Thus this story was born.

While writing, I had trouble with choosing the spelling of names. In Croatian, we use diacritics—my surname, for example, is spelled Mežnarić, not Meznaric. For clarity and ease of reading I choose to transcribe Šimun (spelled with a *Š*) to Shimun (how you would read the *Š* letter). The Shenoa mentioned in the novella is also Šenoa, just like the publisher Shtriga is spelled *Štriga* in Croatian. Also, the *nj* in *Sanja* is a digraph, pronounced similarly to the Spanish *ñ*. *Sanja* also means 'he or she is dreaming' in Croatian.

Another thing that was hard to translate was the Croatian school system. But I asked around among my English language teacher friends and used their advice. I have no idea where teachers in other countries grade papers, but here in Croatia, it's pretty normal to take the job home with us after giving lectures.

Big thanks to my editor and partner in crime Vesna Kurilić, who did an awesome job pointing out where I'd gone too far and helping with my grammar. I couldn't have done this without her.

If you've got a minute of your time and have something to share about the book, honest reviews on Goodreads and social media are appreciated. Word of mouth helps books reach their audience better than anything else out there. Thank you for reading!

ABOUT THE AUTHOR

Antonija is a writer, editor, conrunner and speculative fiction fan. She especially likes horror, urban fantasy and fairy tale retellings. Most of her published works are short stories in Croatian, but you can check out her short sapphic horror story in English, *Of Monsters and Dogs*, for free at shtriga.com.

She also works in the Croatian school system which gives her a plethora of inspiration for horror stories.

You can follow her book ramblings at her haunted site, hauntednarratives.com, or check out her Twitter and Instagram @antonijamezni.

ALSO BY ANTONIJA

Mistress of Geese

A collection of queer folk horror stories about isolation, loneliness, destructive powers of nature, magic and creatures lurking in the dark. Find *Mistress of Geese* on all major retailers.

Of Monsters and Dogs

Who's that lurking in the dark when you're walking your dog at night? Danijela, the heroine in this free short story on shtriga.com, sets out to find out the answer—so we don't have to.

ABOUT SHTRIGA

Hidden stories in your pocket!

Sci fi, fantasy and horror on the go. Publishing your daily dose of speculative fiction since 2020.

Visit

www.shtriga.com

for more information, or follow us

@shtrigabooks

on social for news, upcoming releases, giveaways and more

CPSIA information can be obtained
at www.ICGtesting.com
Printed in the USA
LVHW012149150922
728490LV00003B/540

9 789538 360060